To My Professor: Student Voices for Great College Teaching

What college students really say about their instructors, with advice from master educators and teacher trainers

**Michigan State University
School of Journalism**

For more information and further discussion, visit
http://news.jrn.msu.edu/tomyprofessor

Cover art and design by
Rick Nease
www.RickNeaseArt.com

Published By
Read The Spirit Books
an imprint of
David Crumm Media, LLC
42015 Ford Rd., Suite 234
Canton, Michigan, USA

For information about customized editions, bulk purchases
or permissions, contact David Crumm Media, LLC at info@
DavidCrummMedia.com

This book is dedicated with humble gratitude
to college instructors everywhere
who put their students first.

Contents

Acknowledgments

The authors, from left, front row: Bryce Airgood, Meaghan Markey, Kelly Gooch, Erin Merlo and Alexandria Drzazgowski. Middle row: Nichole Igwe, Christina Briones, Nicole Kazyak, Natalie Kozma, Brittany Dreon and Andrew DiFilippo. Back row: Matthew Hus, Molly Jensen, Hannah Watts, Palak Sabbineni, Michelle Armstead and Eric Straughn. Not shown: Kim Al-Shatel.

We wish to thank the many students who gave us their perspectives and the professors who advocate for great teaching. Some provided strategies for this book and we hope they are among our readers.

We benefited from the work and insight of many allies and advisers. They included the following people from Michigan State University:

Stephen Yelon, professor emeritus in the Michigan State University Department of Counseling, Special Education and Educational Psychology. He consulted in advance of the project and gave it a thorough edit, elevating it in so many ways. From 1969 to 1981, Yelon was assistant director of the Learning and Evaluation Service.

John Bell, director of the MSU Counseling, Educational Psychology and Special Education/College of Education Design Studio and co-coordinator of the Hybrid Educational Psychology and Educational Technology Ph.D. program.

Robert Caldwell, ombudsperson since 2012. He was previously associate chair in the Department of Psychology, associate dean for Graduate Studies in the College of Social Science, and faculty excellence advocate for the College of Social Science.

Maggie Chen Hernandez, associate director of the Office of Cultural & Academic Transitions and senior coordinator for the MOSAIC Multicultural Unity Center and the Intercultural Student Aides.

Deborah DeZure, assistant provost for Faculty and Organizational Development.

Ann Hoffman, assistant dean for undergraduate education, College of Communication Arts and Sciences.

Deana "Dee" Hurlbert, director of the LBGT Resource Center.

Charles "Charlie" Liu, international student adviser/programming in the Office for International Students and Scholars.

Sarah Mellon, veteran resource representative for the Veterans Resource Center.

John Pedraza and **Darryl Steele**, specialists in the Resource Center for Persons with Disabilities.

David Schweikhardt, professor of Agricultural, Food, and Resource Economics.

John L. Sherry, associate dean for graduate studies, College of Communication Arts and Sciences.

Tammison Smith, career advising and training coordinator.

Stan Soffin, ombudsperson from 1998 to 2012 and Journalism School director from 1982 to 1998.

Patti Stewart, director of faculty and instructional development, Office of the Provost.

Several groups also helped. They include the **Intercultural Aides** at Michigan State University, the **TransAction** student group, the **Consortium of Michigan Veterans Educators** and members of the **Student Veterans of America**.

The cover and photo illustration are by **Rick Nease**.

Lead copy editors were Airgood and Kozma. Editing students Natasha Blakely, Meg Dedyne, Alexandra Donlin, Julie Dunmore, Ally Hamzey, Alexis Howell, Lauren Shields and Meghan Steingold also helped.

Kiana Elkins and Stacy Cornwell helped with social media.

The idea of a book about teaching from the student's point of view was conceived at a meeting in the College of Communication Arts and Sciences. Journalism professor Howard Bossen suggested it be created by a class in which students publish 100-question guides to cultural competence. Several of those guides are in this book as resources. Kami Silk, associate dean of research and director of the Master's program in Health and Risk Communications, wrote the proposal for the project. It was accepted by Paulette Granberry Russell, senior adviser to the president for diversity, and director of the Office for Inclusion and Intercultural Initiatives. Denver teacher Kyle Schwartz, creator of the "I Wish My Teacher Knew" project, advised us. Lucinda Davenport, professor and director of the School of Journalism, has supported and advised the project every step of the way.

Preface

"To My Professor: Student Voices for Great College Teaching" matches student opinions about college teaching with advice from master educators and experts. This is not a policy manual or a critique of college instruction. It is not a script for political correctness or a list of banished words. It uses student voices as trailheads for short journeys to better college teaching. The trails are rocky. Rapid changes in content, technology, the student population and the mission of higher education make teaching a challenge.

The students who created this book decided on the sections after gathering statements from other students. The statements were gleaned from many sources. The authors asked other students to complete the phrase "To my professor…" expressing what they might wish to tell professors but felt they could not say directly. The professor-student power differential discourages direct suggestions and drives some students to the anonymity of evaluation forms and social media. We encouraged honesty and minimized harm by respecting the confidentiality of students and instructors involved in friction points.

The authors solicited "To my professor" statements during interviews, on file cards and by email. We mined Twitter, Facebook and other social media. We chose comments for their honesty, relevance and reflection of issues that professors can address, especially in the classroom or lecture hall. We edited some statements for mechanics and length, as we would want anyone to do for us. We preserved the meanings. The authors then sought strategies from exemplary instructors and the people and institutions that helped them get that way.

We envision the audience for this book as college instructors who are dedicated to teaching, who want to understand students better and who are perpetually reinventing themselves. This book is part of a large body of literature about college teaching, but is one of the few that starts with the students.

The book includes practical strategies that align with learning objectives. We include resources for more ideas. "To My Professor" is not linear. You can skip around, picking out the parts that you need based on what is happening at the moment. Keep the book nearby so it's easy to find when new challenges arise, as they most certainly will.

We encourage you to leave comments or look for those by students at http://news.jrn.msu.edu/tomyprofessor/.

To My Colleagues

By Joe Grimm

As educators, we know learning and change can be uncomfortable. Some "To My Professor" statements in this book should make us feel uneasy. Some may seem harsh, one-sided or unfair. Faculty who saw some of the students' statements as the book was being written reacted: "No, that did not happen!" "They got upset about that?" "They don't understand." "That's the exception." Denial is a defense response hard-wired into all of us since well before Confucius and Plato. We don't like to feel attacked.

When you opened this book, you showed that you want to know what students think, no matter what. And you will find some hero stories among the horror stories.

As college instructors, we have many channels for telling students what to do and how to do it. We lecture, we assign, we email, we test, we check, we grade and we meet with them one-on-one. We write the syllabi. We make the rules. When we want to send students a message, we professors communicate through fire hoses. In contrast, students have only squirt guns to fire back at us. This project gives students another channel. But we did not just want you to get a little wet. So, we added strategies from other professors. In the end, most college students and instructors all want great teaching, and we all respect the power of dialogue. So here it is.

When we go into our classrooms and lecture halls, we do so with clear objectives and noble intentions. We have our students' best interests at heart. We want to teach our best and send our students off onto successful journeys. But there are bumps in the teaching road: limited time, growing class sizes, student readiness and every kind of technology. There are a thousand demands and distractions, and students see their college experience through millions of different lenses.

Sometimes, it seems that the longer we teach, the more we put into our teaching and the better we get at it, the harder teaching becomes.

Campuses, temples of free thought and speech, are increasingly places where some teachers and students feel they must walk on eggshells. In 2016, the Higher Education Research Institute at the University of California at Los Angeles released its 50th annual survey of first-year college students. The study included 141,189 full-time students attending about 200 four-year universities around the country. About 71 percent of the students said they agreed "colleges should prohibit racist/sexist speech on campus," the highest rate ever for silencing speech. Asked whether "colleges have the right to ban extreme speakers from campus" 43 percent of the students agreed, about twice what it was in the 1960s, 1970s and 1980s when many of today's professors were students. Racist, sexist and extreme speech was not defined in the study, but students seem more ready than ever to shut it down. In contrast, students said in the survey, and have shown on campuses, that they are more willing than they have been in years to demonstrate about their grievances.

A number of our colleagues have reacted in the press that students want to be coddled or feel they have a right to be free from being offended. Some have said that honest teaching means that students should be offended, because the stimulus provokes them to think and question and prepares them for the real world after college.

Instructors are at the fulcrum of this tippy balance between free speech and respectful dialogue. Once-innocent words have new, sinister meanings. Jokes meant to lighten lessons have become leaden storm clouds. To provoke, in the best sense, has become the worst kind of incitement. Our students have a wider range of perspectives and expectations than ever. The embrace of inclusion is growing wider all the time. Yet financial pressures and technology seem to discourage individualized teaching. As hard as we try and as much as we prepare, sometimes, we just screw up. In the moment when the milk is spilled and dozens of students are watching to see how we are going to clean it up, we goof. A comment that would surely help one student is surely wrong for others. Sometimes, when we know we should de-escalate a situation we watch ourselves elevate it. In college classrooms, issues play out on a stage where they are magnified and scrutinized in full view of an audience equipped to record and broadcast the events. No, it is not easy to be a professor, instructor or teaching assistant.

But we hope the articles and resources in this book will help you teach the way you and your students want. Be open to voices you seldom get to hear and that may not actually be directed at you. You won't get many chances to hear what you'll find in "To My Professor."

Joe Grimm joined the Michigan State University School of Journalism as visiting editor in residence in 2008. Prior to that, he spent 32 years at Detroit-area newspapers, most of them as the recruiting and staff development editor for the Detroit Free Press. In that role, he interviewed students on dozens of campuses. Throughout his newspaper career, he was an adjunct instructor at Oakland University. He wishes to thank the thousands of students who have made his teaching and journalism careers fulfilling.

Foreword

By NiCole T. Buchanan, Ph.D.

I start with a single statement that may be difficult to accept.

Bias permeates every aspect of our work with students, staff and our colleagues.

While most of the chapters in this book are from students, I am writing from one faculty member to another because I am in the trenches with you, struggling to address, minimize

and refrain from acting on my bias while juggling the many challenges posed in undergraduate and graduate instruction. Implicit bias has washed over each and every one of us, coating us with a sticky substance we cannot easily wash away and embedding itself within each of our hearts and minds. It is a simple, yet uncomfortable, truth.

Implicit bias warrants its own dedicated section placed strategically in the front of the book because bias is not constrained to our work with any particular group of students or situations. Implicit bias extends beyond interactions influenced by race or gender and connects to our more subdued beliefs about social class, gender expression, physical abilities, intelligence, standardized tests, age, parent status ... and the list goes on and on. Implicit bias is even present in our beliefs about what constitutes education, learning and their evaluation. As such, this section is highlighted to provide a scaffold for your consideration of the rest of the chapters and a lens through which you can consider your own, and your students', experiences and interactions within higher education.

What is implicit bias?

Bias can be explicit or implicit. Explicit bias is conscious, a preference for one thing over another. In the context of negative bias about other people, explicit bias is similar to old-fashioned -isms (racism, sexism, heterosexism, classism). Studies show that explicit bias has been decreasing in the United States over the past 50 years while *implicit* bias has been increasing during this same timeframe (Pearson, Dovido & Gaertner, 2009).

A critical distinction between explicit and implicit bias is that the latter is outside of our conscious awareness, making it difficult to identify our implicit biases, control their impact on our behavior, or consciously challenge ourselves to rise above them.

Research shows that implicit bias:

- Is pervasive and universal: Everyone has implicit biases and most of us, even members of the groups targeted for bias, harbor the same implicit biases.
- Influences behavior: Implicit bias better predicts actual behaviors than explicit bias, particularly microaggressions and subtle behaviors.
- Impacts life outcomes: Implicit bias results in systematic benefits for some and disadvantages for others.
- Can contradict our explicit beliefs: While honestly believing positives about a group, individuals can simultaneously hold negative implicit biases that influence their behavior toward that group.
- Is costly for all members of society: Both privileged and marginalized group members pay a high price for implicit bias.

- Is malleable: Studies consistently show that efforts to increase our awareness of our biases and challenge ourselves to be conscious and aware of them in our daily interactions can limit the extent to which they impact our behavior and can reduce implicit bias over time.

Diversity fosters academic excellence

Students educated in culturally diverse classrooms demonstrate greater cognitive flexibility, enhanced creativity, improved problem-solving and better utilization of conflict resolution (Gurin et al., 2004; Holoien et al., 2011). These skills are essential for future leaders in our increasingly diverse global economy (Banks, 2015). Educational environments replete with implicit bias reduce the engagement, performance and contribution of diverse students and faculty, resulting in all students losing the benefits associated with a diverse learning environment.

What students want and need from faculty

Students yearn for faculty leadership in addressing implicit bias and moderating difficult conversations around bias and the resulting microaggressions, discrimination and harassment that follow from bias. They are adamant that they want faculty to notice and to act on these events when they occur in the classroom (Harwood et al., 2015). Although a thorough list of suggested best practices for reducing bias in higher education teaching and mentoring is beyond the scope of this section, there are some initial steps that can be useful.

1. Students need faculty to be aware of their own biases and do the work necessary to reduce them. One way to do this is to take several versions of Harvard's Implicit Association Test (IAT) to increase your awareness of which domains you have biases about and how strong your biases are in that area (links to the IAT are below).

2. Address implicit bias when it occurs in the classroom. Regardless of whether you teach physics, history, geology, art, psychology or music, you can use your

classroom to create an inclusive learning environment. Learn how to facilitate difficult conversations generally and the nuances of these conversations around diversity in particular. As leaders in the classroom, it is our responsibility to speak the hard truths, ask the difficult questions, reward courage, and to identify, question, and correct for implicit bias in our curriculum, instruction and classroom interactions.

3. Resist "color blindness" and "other blindness." Color blindness refers to the denial of racial, ethnic or cultural differences by emphasizing how people are the same and implying that differences are not important (Neville et al., 2013). Although often well-intentioned, color- or other-blindness endorse the status quo, which perpetuate the marginalization of some and privileging of others (Banks, K. H., 2014).

4. Invest in your personal education on implicit bias. Below are several resources as beginning steps to increasing your understanding of implicit bias, its harmful impact on students, and the steps you can take to reduce its influence in your classrooms. In addition, many college campuses and surrounding communities have reading and discussion groups around these concerns and group trainings are available to learn how to better address bias in higher education.

Why commit to reducing implicit bias in higher education?

Research indicates that although it can be difficult, there are considerable benefits to actively working to reduce implicit bias in the workplace and in institutions of higher education.

These are some benefits of implicit bias training and interventions:

- Increases commitment, retention, and satisfaction with one's major/career choice

- Improves camaraderie, department climate, student/faculty/employee morale
- Capitalizes on student/faculty talent, ideas and collaborative problem-solving
- Reduces conflict
- Strengthens teams, improves trust
- Enhances student and faculty physical health and psychological well-being
- Strengthens community and campus relationships
- Increases individuals' confidence in their actions in the classroom and workplace

NiCole Buchanan, Ph.D., is an associate professor in the Department of Psychology at Michigan State University. Her research focuses on the interplay of race, gender and victimization, racialized sexual harassment, and how social identity dimensions, such as race, gender, sexual orientation and social class relate to well-being and professional development. Buchanan is a fellow of the American Psychological Association and has received several honors and awards for her research and teaching. Buchanan provides diversity-related training and consultation to academic departments and organizations, including academic and practicing psychologists, human resource managers and campus, city and state police departments.

References and resources

Banks, James A. "Cultural Diversity and Education." New York: Routledge, 2015.

Banks, Kira Hudson. "'Perceived' Discrimination as an Example of Color-blind Racial Ideology's Influence on Psychology." American Psychologist, 69, 311–313, 2014.

Carnes, Molly, et al. "Promoting Institutional Change Through Bias Literacy." Journal of Diversity in Higher Education, 5, 63-77, 2012.

Dasgupta, Nilanjana. "Implicit Attitudes and Beliefs Adapt to Situations: A Decade of Research on the Malleability of Implicit Prejudice, Stereotypes, and the Self-concept." Advances in Experimental Social Psychology, 47, 233-279, 2013.

Equality Challenge Unit. "Unconscious Bias in Higher Education." 2013. http://www.ecu.ac.uk/publications/unconscious-bias-in-higher-education/

Glicksman, Eve. "Unconscious Bias in Academic Medicine: Overcoming the Prejudices We Don't Know We Have." Association of American Medical Colleges, 2016.

Greenwald, Anthony G., and Linda Hamilton Krieger. "Implicit Bias: Scientific Foundations." California Law Review, 94(4), 945-967, 2006.

Gurin, Patricia, and Biren (Ratnesh) A. Nagda. "Getting to the What, How, and Why of Diversity on Campus." Educational Researcher, 35(1), 20-24, 2006.

Harvard's Implicit Association Test (IAT)

https://implicit.harvard.edu/implicit/takeatest.html

https://implicit.harvard.edu/implicit/iatdetails.html

Harwood, Stacy Anne, Shinwoo Choi, Moises Orozco, Margaret Browne Huntt, and Ruby Mendenhall. "Racial Microaggressions at the University of Illinois at Urbana-Champaign: Voices of Students of Color in the Classroom."

University of Illinois at Urbana-Champaign, 2015. http://www.racialmicroaggressions.illinois.edu/

Holoien, Deborah Son, and J. Nicole Shelton. "You Deplete Me: The Cognitive Costs of Colorblindness on Ethnic Minorities." Journal of Experimental Social Psychology, 48(2), 562-565, 2011. doi: 10.1016/j.jesp.2011.09.010.

Hurtado, Sylvia. "Linking Diversity with the Educational and Civic Missions of Higher Education." The Review of Higher Education, 30(2), 185-196, 2007.

Johnson, Allan G. "Privilege, Power and Difference," 2nd ed. Boston: McGraw Hill, 2005.

Kirwan Institute. "2015 State of the Science: Implicit Bias Review." http://kirwaninstitute.osu.edu/my-product/2015-state-of-the-science-implicit-bias-review/

Neville, Helen A., et al. "Color-blind Racial Ideology: Theory, Training, and Measurement Implications in Psychology." American Psychologist, 68, 455–466, 2013. doi:10.1037/a0033282.

Pearson, Adam R., John F. Dovidio, and Samuel L. Gaertner. "The Nature of Contemporary Prejudice: Insights from Aversive Racism." Social and Personality Psychology Compass, 3(3), 314-338, 2009.

Stevens, Flannery G., Victoria C. Plaut, and Jeffrey Sanchez-Burks. "Unlocking the Benefits of Diversity. All-Inclusive Multiculturalism and Positive Organizational Change." The Journal of Applied Behavioral Science, 44(1), 116-133, 2008.

Stone, Jeff, and Gordon B. Moskowitz. "Non-conscious Bias in Medical Decision Making: What Can Be Done to Reduce it?" Medical Education, 45(8), 768-76, 2011.

Sue, Derald Wing. "Microaggressive Impact on Education and Teaching: Facilitating Difficult Dialogues on Race in the Classroom." In D. W. Sue (ed.), "Microaggressions in Everyday Life: Race, Gender, and Sexual Orientation." Hoboken: John Wiley & Sons, 231-254, 2010.

Tarca, Katherine. "Colorblind in Control: The Risks of Resisting Difference Amid Demographic Change." Educational Studies, 38(2), 99-120, 2005.

Worthington, Roger L., Rachel L. Navarro, Michael Loewy, and Jenni Hart. "Color-Blind Racial Attitudes, Social Dominance Orientation, Racial-ethnic Group Membership and College Students' Perceptions of Campus Climate." Journal of Diversity in Higher Education, 1(1), 8-19, 2008.

Yap, Margaret, Mark Robert Holmes, Charity-Ann Hannan, and Wendy Cukier. "The Relationship Between Diversity Training, Organizational Commitment, and Career Satisfaction." Journal of European Industrial Training, 34(6), 519-538, 2010.

Structures and syllabi

The syllabus: Road map for a smooth experience

"Why make a syllabus if you're not going to follow anything that's on it?"

"My professor just gave us the class syllabus and class has been in session for 5 weeks."

"My English professor didn't give us a syllabus, So disorganized smh. I already forgot what pages we're supposed to read in a book I don't have."

Most professors have had a student misunderstand an assignment or due date, or challenge a grade. Clear guidelines, deadlines and communication can help prevent that.

The syllabus is one of the most important documents a professor gives to students, yet they can become long, disorganized and out of date. Some students don't look at them; some professors seem to just recycle the old ones. A syllabus is not a contract, but it is a method to convey the professor's encouragement and expectations and what students can expect in return.

Researchers for the Association of Psychological Science report that when professors fail to follow the syllabus during the term, students can perceive them to be careless and disorganized. Students are also more likely to highlight negative in-class experiences in end-of-term evaluations. Some administrators say a chief complaint they see is that a course lacks organization.

Ellen Bremen, author of "Say This, NOT That to Your Professor: 36 Talking Tips for College Success," cited on her blog an email from a student. In it, the student wrote the professor had changed the grading scale and syllabus at the end of the term, causing a student's grade to drop from a C+ to a D, forcing that student to retake the course. The student wrote: "I went to the department head and the dean and they both told me they were siding with the professor and if I filed a formal grade challenge, the same people that turned me away would be the ones deciding the final grade in the formal challenge process. What can I do?"

Strategies

Stephen Yelon, professor emeritus in the Department of Counseling, Special Education and Educational Psychology at Michigan State University, advises professors to keep the purpose of a syllabus in mind when setting its tone. The syllabus is a road map to success and can encourage the student to achieve that. Just as potholes can disrupt a smooth driving experience, a negative tone of a syllabus can be detrimental to students' perception of both the professor and the course. "It's like a letter from you to your students to orient them to the course and to give them information that will help them learn and succeed. As such, write the syllabus using a friendly, supportive tone."

In a handout he revised in 2013 called "The Best Syllabus Ever! Checklist of Possible Elements in a Syllabus," Yelon wrote, "Use words like 'I will provide time for you to see me personally so that I may help you be successful…' rather than 'the instructor's hours are from 2-3 on alternate Tuesdays …' Positively worded phrases like 'When you arrive late, please seat yourself so that you minimize distraction of your classmates…' prove more effective than 'Lateness will not be tolerated.'"

According to the Teaching and Learning Transformation Center at the University of Maryland, "Your syllabus tells your students what your course is about, what the learning objectives are, and the ways a student can be successful in your course. A complete and well-designed syllabus can help set the tone for a positive teaching and learning environment and acts as a contract that clearly details both student and instructor responsibilities."

While the syllabus is not a legal contract, it should not be changed casually or unilaterally. In her book "Becoming a New Instructor: A Guide for College Adjuncts and Graduate Students," Erika Falk advises, "Do not plan to change your syllabus mid-class unless something is going dramatically wrong. Instead, make a copy of your syllabus and make the changes to that version so that you remember, but only put them into effect the next time you teach."

Clean, effective design is also important to creating attractive, readable syllabi. It should be easy for students to skim through quickly to find due dates, required texts, grading procedures and resources. Anyone can design syllabi effectively, keeping in mind consistent and proper use of headings, white space, indentation, bold and italics.

Most universities suggest that policy and resource items be added or appended to the syllabus and those sections may be based on previous documents. But clarity, consistency and a little enthusiasm expressed in a syllabus can really make a difference in how the course goes and how students perceive it.

Resources

Falk, Erika. "Becoming a New Instructor: A Guide for College Adjuncts and Graduate Students." New York: Routledge, 2012.

Rosen, Lois, ed. "Syllabus Design." Michigan State University Office of Faculty and Organizational Development, http://fod.msu.edu/oir/syllabus-design

Yelon, Stephen L. "Powerful Principles of Instruction." White Plains: Longman USA, 1996.

—Hannah Watts is a journalism major and public relations minor.

Don't serve lessons after their freshness dates

"I had a professor who didn't update his slides between semesters. He was teaching information that might not be correct anymore because the data was over 10 years old."

"I had a professor who was telling the class something and trying to get us to relate to it and I was 18 and I was like, 'man, I just don't understand what you're saying."

Concepts, principles and values don't change overnight; theories, examples and student perspectives can. Effective teaching requires constant refreshing to stay current and relevant. Failure to update allows lessons and lectures to become irrelevant or outdated. Consequently, the lessons lose their appeal. In addition to content changes, a teacher might consider updates to cultural references and other milestones, as each new generation of students has a different frame of reference.

Depending on their fields, it can be difficult for some professors to keep material fresh and up to date. Some disciplines require annual updates, while others might require a more consistent base.

Sometimes students feel uncomfortable learning older material. Some are willing to do so if they feel the facts, concepts and principles are still relevant, but students need to be able to see the significance to understand why the material is important. They also need to know if they, too, are allowed to use out-of-date material in their work.

- One student said she had a science professor who would use material that was both old and new. The student felt like these different sources were good in some ways, but she was confused because she was not allowed to use older material in papers. "Both were beneficial, but it was confusing. He would say don't use material from before this date, but then he would use material from before this date," she said. She felt it was unfair that she couldn't use articles before the "acceptable" date as the professor did.

- Students are thinking about their futures and want to learn new things, so if they feel the material is old, they feel like they won't learn what they need. Students tweet about material being old or irrelevant. One student wrote, "This teacher brought VHS tapes to class. I'm sure the material on them is completely relevant to today's marketing world (rolling eyes emoji.)" In contrast, students enjoy a class when they feel professors are teaching topics they think the students want to learn. As one student wrote, "Basically I think it's cool when professors keep class material relevant to what we want to know more about."

- Students sometimes are annoyed or unsure about the accuracy of older materials presented in class. One psychology major said that it "bugged" her when professors used facts that were more than three or four years old. Another psychology major said one of his statistics classes kept citing the 2000 census, years after the 2010 results came out.

Strategies

How can professors know what material students will see as relatable and relevant?

A Stanford University faculty newsletter described ways to keep lessons fresh. These are some practices faculty said worked for them:

- Attend or organize teaching lunches or retreats with colleagues to exchange syllabi and teaching ideas.
- Take notes about the course during the semester and analyze student evaluations right after the course as a way of generating ideas for change. Read the feedback before redesigning the course or teaching it again.

- Commit to one pedagogical change a year. Use iTunes, break lectures into discussions, or ask questions for students to answer in pairs.
- Learn from students. Let them be the experts on new technology.
- Let TAs play an active role in the course. They can be an invaluable resource for new materials, ideas and technology.

Michael Kohen, an adjunct professor in the English Department at Lansing Community College in Michigan, developed a strategy for keeping his material relevant and relatable for students.

He casts his net for material back no further than 10 years. Anything older than 10 years, unless it was truly spectacular, he would not use. Kohen teaches a freshman writing course where most of his students are 18 or 19. They were only 8 or 9 years old at the time the material was published, so older events and references might be hard for them to remember, let alone relate to.

"Anything that happened in the last 10 years I feel like I can comfortably discuss," Kohen said. "I stopped really talking about 9/11 because my students, I mean … they don't even remember 9/11."

Kohen said a colleague uses Ted Talks videos to teach his classes. Kohen said this method is great for today's students.

"This is not someone who probably grew up listening to podcasts or watching things on YouTube, but has found this way to communicate with students and make connections with them through the Ted Talks that I think is amazing," Kohen said. "That's the kind of innovation I think makes for a great professor."

Resources

Hai-Jew, Shalin. "An Instructional Design Approach to Updating an Online Course Curriculum." Educause, 2010. June 12, 2016. http://er.educause.edu/articles/2010/12/an-instructional-design-approach-to-updating-an-online-course-curriculum

"Keeping It Fresh—Maintaining the Jazz in Teaching: A Panel Discussion with Stanford Faculty." Stanford University Center for Learning and Teaching, 2008. June 12, 2016. http://web.stanford.edu/dept/CTL/Newsletter/keeping_fresh.pdf

Mellow, Gail, et al. "Taking College Teaching Seriously: Pedagogy Matters! Fostering Student Success through Faculty Centered Practice Improvement." Sterling: Stylus Publishing, LLC, 2015.

—Bryce Airgood is a journalism major.

The doctor is in: Making office hours count

"You told us you were always available to us when we needed help, but every time I tried to schedule a time to meet, you would come up with an excuse."

"There were many times more than I can count on my hand when I set up office hours with my professor and he didn't show up or was busy after he already gave me a certain time to meet him. If the teacher is not going to follow through with his own expectations, then how can you expect your students to respect you, let alone want to be in your class?"

There are two occasions when college instructors are asked to commit specific times to students: teaching hours and office hours.

Classes and labs are structured events that rarely change. Office hours, less so.

Some professors complain that students seldom attend office hours, or they appear without any real purpose. Interest in visiting the office rises later in the term when students want to talk about grades, but until then, office hours can become a time to prepare for class, catch up on grading or make other appointments. Some students say they get used to finding the door closed and the professor unavailable during office hours.

Office hours may be posted outside office doors, or written in syllabi, but when no one is in at those times, students feel like teachers have broken their commitment. One student tweeted, "These professors want you to come see them but when you try to make an appointment with them, they're unavailable. #HateSchool."

Another student reported feeling frustrated and helpless. When students don't understand something in class and can't get help, they fall behind and lose interest in going to class. Hearing the professor take a lesson further down a road students aren't on compounds the frustration and the feeling of being left behind.

A college student posted on Twitter, "My terrible, horrible, very bad, no-good marketing professor decided that he's just gonna make himself unavailable until the test. #help."

There must be a better answer for both students and instructors.

Strategies

Ann Hoffman is the assistant dean for undergraduate education in the Michigan State University College of Communication Arts and Sciences. Hoffman said that, just like providing students with a clear syllabus, it is the faculty's responsibility to be available to help students overcome problems. Office hours are a mechanism for that. Phone calls and emails are an option if office hours don't align for student and teacher.

David Gooblar, a lecturer in the rhetoric department at the University of Iowa, wrote in a column on Vitae that professors should require students to meet with them privately.

"Meeting with students one-on-one allows us to be better teachers, to reach students more effectively, regardless of whether the meetings lead to higher grades," Gooblar said.

Students may feel more comfortable privately asking questions that they do not want to ask in class.

Margaret Walsh, a sociology professor at Keene State College in New Hampshire, thinks about office hours in terms of minutes. Three hours per week in a 15-week semester yields 2,700 minutes. This is time Walsh wants to use well. She starts by trying to pick times that maximize the number of students who can meet her during office hours.

She recommends three different weekdays, and doesn't rule out virtual office hours at other times.

Some of her other recommendations are about setting the stage for a good, uncluttered conversation. Walsh also advises listening and collaborating and sharing books or other resources with students who come to learn. She writes that students show up, and that office conversations can alleviate classroom problems.

How will you use your 2,700 minutes?

Resources

Gooblar, David. "Make Your Office Hours a Requirement." Vitae, the Online Career Hub for Higher Ed., Chronicle of Higher Education, 2015. June 12, 2016 https://chroniclevitae.com/news/1167-make-your-office-hours-a-requirement

Walsh, Margaret. "Seven Ways to Make Office Hours Better for Students." Faculty Focus, Higher Ed Teaching Strategies from Magna Publications, 2011. June 12, 2016 http://www.facultyfocus.com/articles/teaching-and-learning/how-to-make-the-most-of-your-office-hours/

—Nicole Kazyak is a communication major and public relations minor.

Civility means knowing and respecting your audience

"Don't worry, professor, I'll remember how rude you were to me when I asked you for help when I fill out your class evaluation form."

"It's incredibly rude to cancel the first class after spring break at 8:20 when class starts at 8:30. I was already on my way."

"I hate it when my entire grade is based off of two exams."

"I hate it when you give a pop quiz when I go to the bathroom."

Successful performers know their audiences and, to teach well, the more professors know about their students, the better. While professors are aware of rules regarding civil conduct by students and write those expectations into their syllabi, civility runs two ways. Students expect professors to respect them, too.

Universities, government, law firms, hospitals and other organizations have seized on the civility concept and given it a wider definition than it has in the dictionary. Civil Politics, a group founded by academics, defines civility as "the ability to disagree productively with others, respecting their sincerity and decency. By civility we do NOT mean agreement. We think citizens are well served when political parties represent different viewpoints and then compete vigorously to recruit voters to their side."

Under some campus definitions, civility goes beyond discussion and covers more general behavior.

According to a training program at the University of Missouri, "Civility is consistently treating people with consideration and respect and valuing the culture and humanity of others."

In contrast, incivility, has come to mean rudeness such as interrupting, and acting disrespectfully. Sometimes professors do not realize their behavior comes across as inconsiderate or inappropriate.

In "The Art & Craft of College Teaching: A Guide for New Professors & Graduate Students," Robert Rotenberg wrote that making classrooms more trusting and supportive elevates student engagement.

He wrote, "You cannot teach effectively if you do not know who your students are–or worse, if you assume they are one kind of learner, when in fact, they are not."

Atmosphere matters. Creating a classroom ambience where students can learn is the key in developing a good relationship and understanding among students and professors.

Some students said a lack of understanding felt like a lack of respect for them.

- One student reported feeling slighted because his professor often gave the class last-minute assignments. "He would just pull stuff out of nowhere that wasn't on the syllabus and expect us to be fine with it," he said. Students may find it difficult to reconcile syllabus issues when they feel professors contradicted their own document.

- An art student recalled waking up one morning to an email from a professor asking her class to do an exercise before class that day. She concluded that her professor thought his class was the only one she was taking. "There was no consideration whatsoever. None at all," she said.

- Students sometimes criticize the rudeness of classmates who talk through lecture or who pack up to leave before the class has ended. They look to professors to reclaim a respectful atmosphere.

Strategies

Assistant communications professor Dustin Carnahan at Michigan State University explained that professors rarely intend to hurt students, but that there can be misunderstandings.

Carnahan said, "If I find something that is immediately relevant to class, I'll share it. I'm hoping that my students have some interest in that topic since they are in the class. I think it is mostly to help them and it can be helpful if students can be more cognizant of the fact that professors are trying to help and not trying to make life harder. I think it's a fine line."

Although it is not the professor's job to diagnose, it is important that professors are open to the possibility that students they might assume are underperforming have a learning disability. Rotenberg suggests that professors educate themselves about learning disabilities to the extent that they know the right questions to ask of an underperforming student.

Another civility issue is how receptive professors are to student concerns. Rotenberg wrote, "Careful attention to their complaints is an important part of enhancing the learning experience. Instead of dismissing these complaints or asserting your authority to construct the classroom any way you wish, consider the strength of commitment to goals and priorities that students are describing when they complain."

Sensitivity can be key when emotions or behaviors take center stage. Professors can let students express themselves and vent their frustrations. The professor can set ground rules, offer a listening ear, affirmation and a possible solution, but not judgment.

Rotenberg wrote, "Your first response in these situations should be the humane one … Unless you believe the student may be making something up, you can dispense with asking the student for proof."

A 2014 study by the University of Minnesota's Student Conflict Resolution Center defined academic harassment as "hostile, intimidating, or threatening behavior which interferes with the ability to work or study." It found that while the number of graduate students reporting such behavior was on the rise, it was usually not reported. Forty-two percent of those who reported harassment said their statement led to retaliation. Reported or not, even mild incivility can take a toll. One student wrote, "There needs to be some sort of people management class for professors ... These skills often get overlooked as 'soft' skills that can be learned on the job and that are nice but not necessary, but the truth is that those skills are the most difficult to learn. Without mastery of these skills, the productivity of a lab can be severely impeded."

Several universities publish techniques for ensuring civility. The University of Missouri offers a toolbox and links to other resources with advice to help professors model civility and squelch incivility.

Some ideas from the Missouri toolbox:

- Tone of voice matters.
- Work collaboratively with your class, colleagues and friends to define and apply respectful behaviors.
- Have difficult conversations in person or, at a minimum, by telephone, not electronically.
- Understand your triggers or "hot buttons." Knowing what makes you angry and frustrated helps you manage your reactions and respond more appropriately.

In the end, an instructor's role may be reflected by the students. Inflexibility and insensitivity breed inflexibility and insensitivity. Nobody wins.

But if teachers take the time to know their audiences and to jointly create an atmosphere of support and trust, students will meet the professor halfway. Then everybody wins.

Resources

Rotenberg, Robert Louis. "The Art & Craft of College Teaching: A Guide for New Professors & Graduate Students." Walnut Creek: Left Coast, 2010.

"Show Me Respect: Civility Toolbox." University of Missouri-Columbia Show Me Respect Steering Committee. June 12, 2016 http://civility.missouri.edu/committee.php

—*Nichole Igwe is a journalism major and a public relations and French minor.*

Going beyond grades to feedback and growth

"If my professor doesn't hurry up and post my grade for the paper that took me many 3 a.m. nights to do, then I'm going to have a stroke."

"Man, my professor didn't grade my first paper that I turned in 3 months ago."

"What type of professor gives you a bad grade on a paper and the only comments written were 'incorrect use of a semicolon' and 'good.'"

"Three weeks left in semester, professor realizes we only have 1 grade. Adds a paper, 2 assignments & observation research project."

There is one malady that students and instructors all suffer: grade anxiety.

In an article for the National Association of Scholars, George Leef nailed the instructor's perspective: "Anyone who has taught a college course knows the problems that come with the need to assign grades: the excuses, the pleading, the close-calls, the possibility of causing trouble for yourself, and so on."

At Michigan State University, students can take complaints about grades to the Ombudsperson's Office, the first such office in the country. According to Ombudsman Robert Caldwell's report to the president for the 2014-2015 academic year, 79 percent of student contacts had to do with academic issues, driven largely by issues of academic dishonesty and grades. While the number of students who make formal complaints about grades is small, many more take to social media when they feel grades are late, unfair, unexplained or when graded work is assigned without warning.

Angela Duckworth, a professor of psychology at the University of Pennsylvania and a 2013 MacArthur fellow, joked that grades make her "feel like I need legal counsel when I write my syllabus." She said this just after addressing the 2016 seminar of the Education Writers Association in Boston.

It was the morning before the release of her book "Grit: The Power of Passion and Perseverance."

Duckworth suggested that instructors try to move the focus from grades to feedback to make the process more helpful, and possibly curb the anxiety, the challenges and the complaints.

Strategies

Duckworth, founder and scientific director of Penn's Character Lab, recommended more feedback, not less, and said college students are relatively starved for it. She said students graduate from high school, where they might get grades every week, then go to college, where they might get as few as one at mid-term and another at the end of the course. Then, after they graduate, they go to work where they get no grades, but might get feedback on their work every day.

Duckworth recommends professors tell students how they are doing much more frequently.

Scores of researchers have investigated whether more frequent feedback helps students and the consensus is that, yes, more frequent assessments generally help students achieve. Side benefits of more frequent, less weighted tests are better attendance, less pressure on finals and better opinions by students about the course and instructor.

Duckworth further suggested that grades be used as incentives to use the feedback. She said professors get frustrated when students look for the grade but ignore the feedback and keep repeating old mistakes. So, she suggests incentives to get students to learn from the feedback. Grades can become motivational if there are opportunities to raise them by using feedback to improve.

Another incentive to improve performance is social pressure, Duckworth said. If students know their work will be reviewed by others, such as peers who rate their work, they will use feedback to look better.

In a column for Vitae, David Gooblar wrote, "grading isn't going to go away anytime soon, alas. So it is worth trying to think differently about this hated part of our work lives." Gooblar is a lecturer in the rhetoric department at the University of Iowa. He distinguishes between graded summative judgments, which say how well students perform, and feedback or formative assessments intended to improve performance. He, too, recommends early and frequent feedback.

Gooblar wrote that students who get helpful feedback early are more likely to feel that their professors are treating them like individuals, and want them to progress. When they agreed with the feedback, they said they worked harder to meet the professor's expectations.

As a new associate professor at Appalachian State University, Michael Howell realized through comments from his students that his feedback to them was not helping. So, he consulted the literature.

Howell summarized the literature on feedback in five points, with citations, for an article in the Journal on Excellence in College Teaching.

Writer Geoff Decker described Howell's experience and strategies for the Association of College and University Educators.

Howell's recommendations are:

- Be timely with feedback: This helps students do better on the next assignment. (It also saves professors from being overwhelmed when work piles up.)
- Be balanced: Cite specific hits and misses and tie them to learning objectives. Sarcasm and cheers don't do that.
- Focus on development: Connect feedback to future job performance.

- Be direct: No hedging. Howell advised against "sugaring the pill," a phrase he borrowed from researchers.
- Instruct: Identify issues, explain them and tell how to avoid them.

Resources

Decker, Geoff. "Research Roundup: Five Principles for Giving Effective Feedback to Students." ACUE Community Site Wide Activity RSS. The Association of College and University Educators, 2016. June 12, 2016 https://community.acue.org/blog/research-roundup-five-principles-effective-written-feedback-to-students/

Gooblar, David. "Student Feedback Matters-and It Goes Beyond Grading." Vitae, the Online Career Hub for Higher Ed., Chronicle of Higher Education, 2014. June 12, 2016 https://chroniclevitae.com/news/392-student-feedback-matters-and-it-goes-beyond-grading

—Joe Grimm is visiting editor in residence in the School of Journalism.

Student safety matters on and off campus

"I really appreciated when you wanted to talk to me about why I was crying outside of class. I was having major issues with my roommate that made me feel unsafe, and it impacted every aspect of my life. Personal lives are usually kept separate from college classes, but you did everything you could to make sure I was OK. Having professors that care makes campus feel like a safe space."

"It made me feel safe and cared for when my professor told the class that they were available for anyone that needs someone to talk to after another mass shooting had just occurred on a different campus. It reminded me how much professors can care for their students."

Most college students are on their own, maybe for the first time, so professors might be the only caring adults they interact with on a regular basis. Professors try to control what happens in the classroom, and even that is not easy, but cannot control the outside world. Still, professors know that outside factors affect classroom performance and watch for signs of distress.

Students face all kinds of abuse, grief or addiction that can put them at risk. According to the Centers of Disease Control and Prevention these are issues affecting the health and safety of students:

- Suicide is the third leading cause of death among persons aged 15-24.
- One in five women college women have been sexually assaulted
- About 90 percent of the alcohol consumed by people under the age of 21 is in the form of binge drinking.
- In 2013, around 21 percent of those aged 18-25 reported use of illicit drugs in the previous month.

All the dangers listed can be major risks to people of college age. Away from home and parental guidance, students can make bad choices or face dangerous situations they cannot handle alone. If a professor notices dramatic changes in behavior, that could be a sign of trouble. A concerned word or a question can start to turn things around for a student.

According to a 2014 Gallup-Purdue Index Report, college students "had double the chances of being engaged in their work and were three times as likely to be thriving in their well-being if they connected with a professor on the campus who stimulated them, and encouraged their hopes and dreams." Professors are not health and safety experts, but reaching out can help students feel safe and cared for. If necessary, professors can make students aware of university resources that can help them.

Sometimes, professors must do more than listen. Policies vary by the institution and the situation. Title IX of the Federal Education Act of 1972 says "No person in the United States shall, on the basis of sex, be excluded from participation in, be denied the benefits of, or be subjected to discrimination under any education program or activity receiving Federal financial assistance." So, some universities have adopted policies that make most faculty members mandatory reporters on issues such as assault and relationship violence.

An Inside Higher Ed article explored the debate over requiring faculty and staff to report offenses such as sexual assault. The concern is that having rules that require professors to be mandatory reporters will make students less likely to confide in them, or they will violate the trust of students who do not want their assault to be investigated and documented. Reporter Colleen Flaherty wrote, "professors in many cases resent the choice with which they are faced: complying with students' wishes about privacy or with their institutions' reporting requirements."

Strategies

Scott Merlo, chief of police and director of security for Western Michigan University, says it is important that professors show students they care about them even outside the classroom. "Being accessible to students by telling them you are there to talk at any time and by getting to know them is a good way to show students you care. The more you get to know a student and their normal behaviors, the easier it is to tell if there is a safety concern," Merlo said.

Changes can be warning signs of a student who is in trouble outside the classroom, he said. "Professors should look for major changes in behavior. If students have trouble getting to class on time or getting to class at all, when that is not usually like them, they could be dealing with something big. If their hygiene turns poor, then there could be a health concern.

Or, if they are just struggling with assignments when they usually do well, it could be a sign of a problem," Merlo said.

Because Title IX policies are set by individual institutions, professors must know the protocol for their campus. These rules are usually posted online and, when an issue arises, the instructor is usually referred to a supervisor or the university Title IX officer. These are the people to ask about responsibilities and the balance between confidentiality and mandatory reporting. Conflicted instructors can have a conversation with a supervisor or administrator to save themselves from working this out alone during an active situation.

Instructors are not responsible for resolving problems and typically don't have the background for that. Assaults, though complicated, usually have a straightforward and specific line of communication for mandatory reporters.

Instructors at all levels have a new role in paying attention to students' safety right in their own classroom. Time magazine reported there were 23 campus shootings in 2015. Merlo said there are many ways professors can make the classroom feel safer. First, he encourages professors to "point out exits and escape routes for fire and safety emergencies on the first day of class." This allows students to be aware of their surroundings, and it also shows them that their professors care about their students while they are in their classroom. Many college students have been getting this training since kindergarten, so it should not come as a surprise or a threat.

Students' safety matters wherever they are, and trouble can impact students' lives in and out of the classroom. Professors are sometimes the first to notice there is a problem and the first to point them toward solutions that help.

Resources

Centers for Disease Control and Prevention. "Six Tips for College Health and Safety." June 12, 2016 http://www.cdc.gov/features/collegehealth/

Flaherty, Colleen. "Endangering a Trust." Inside Higher Ed, 2015. June 12, 2016 https://www.insidehighered.com/news/2015/02/04/faculty-members-object-new-policies-making-all-professors-mandatory-reporters-sexual

Kreuter, Nate. "Dealing with Unstable Students." Inside Higher Ed, 2014. 12 Jun 2016 https://www.insidehighered.com/advice/2014/01/08/essay-how-faculty-members-can-respond-unstable-students

—Erin Merlo is a comparative cultures and politics and English major with a minor in public relations. Scott Merlo is her father.

Engaging everyone

Getting the whole class involved

"My stats prof can't pronounce my name so she never calls on me."

"Putting my hand up and then down 3,000 times, as the prof never calls on me."

"My prof tells me I need to participate in class discussions more but every time I raise my hand she never calls on me ... "

The range of personalities in a classroom is remarkable. Some students are "extroverted" and sit in the front row for every class and jump into or start conversations unbidden. Then there are those who hunker down in the back row, avoiding eye contact and engagement. One student sat behind a pillar for every class. Some educators describe their personalities as "avoidant."

Between these two extremes are students who are neither extroverted nor avoidant. They may be reflected in the tweets quoted above.

They might be quiet, shy or hesitant, but they are waiting to be invited in. When it doesn't happen, despite raised hands and other signs, they feel ignored, overlooked and as though they are not on some list of the professor's favorite students.

One teacher was shocked when a former student said he had hated the teacher because he had never been called on. The teacher had liked the student but believed he understood the material and needed no further help or encouragement. The teacher had been focused on other students who were problems in the classroom. This student was no problem. Or so it seemed.

How do professors get more students to engage when some students are jumping right in, others are trying to stay out and it is unclear what the ones in the middle want?

Strategies

Amol Pavangadkar watches for "floaters." This is his term for students he sees floating through his class and keeping low profiles on their way toward graduation, flying under the radar and trying not to attract any attention. Pavangadkar is a senior producer and a specialist with the Department of Media & Information in the Michigan State College of Communication Arts and Sciences. In 2016, he won the college's Faculty Impact Award, which recognizes "faculty members who have changed lives through classroom excellence."

His student load has nearly tripled from about two dozen to 54 spread across three sections of cinema and TV projects. Two of Pavangadkar's strategies seem to be opposites. One is to schedule a time for every student to stand before the class and critique a video portfolio, or a reel, they have found online. Every student has a scheduled opportunity to be the focal point, like it or not. Their grade is not based on their performance, but on the paper they write.

Pavangadkar's second approach takes place outside the classroom with one-on-one meetings to advise students on video projects. Rather than call out the floaters publicly, he has them file time and location plans with him. This allows Pavangadkar to observe their techniques, track progress and give them the privacy and confidentiality they often seek.

He often finds that "some students have undisclosed issues or baggage." These can be mental, physical or legal issues. Sometimes, university offices know about issues, but professors are not informed by either the university or the student. Pavangadkar says learning student backstories helps both parties understand how to work together and get students engaged.

Pavangadkar also tries to meet with each student twice a semester, 10 minutes at a time. He hosts office hours, but finds they are not as effective as appointments and might not be convenient for all of his students' schedules, so he schedules meetings outside of set hours.

An assistant professor in Pavangadkar's department, Rabindra "Robby" Ratan uses a different technique. Pavangadkar tells students to learn from their failures, shares stories of his own defeats and holds a taut line on deadlines. Ratan says he draws energy from his Understanding Media class of 350 students, and he feels like an entertainer. He rolls in on one of his seven skateboards, and glides back and forth at the front of the hall during lectures, drawing students' eyes and attention back and

forth. When he sees a raised hand, especially a new one in the back, Ratan will not just call on the student, he will applaud and cheer.

He calls on students by name and, when he does not know the name, he asks for it, even if he has done so before.

"When I started this I felt kind of awkward. Then I gave myself the maxim to learn as many names as I could," said Ratan.

When he has forgotten a name, he apologizes. "I know you already told me," he says, and he asks again. There is not a cut-off point in the semester when he feels it is too late to ask for a name. He takes responsibility for forgetting and does not embarrass students for lack of participation, saying that "blaming can lead to defensiveness."

Ratan wants to demonstrate that professors are learning, too, and prone to mistakes. From the standpoint of using their own goofs and gaffes as teaching points, Ratan and Pavangadkar are similar.

Ratan credits the Lilly Teaching Fellows Program with some of his teaching success. The program, which is on many campuses, helps junior faculty at many colleges and universities.

Resources

Bean, John C., and Maryellen Weimer. "Engaging Ideas: The Professor's Guide to Integrating Writing, Critical Thinking, and Active Learning in the Classroom." San Francisco: Jossey-Bass, 2011.

Roehling, Patricia Vincent, et al. "Engaging the Millennial Generation in Class Discussions." College Teaching 59.1 (2010): 1-6. College Teaching. Taylor & Francis Ltd., 2011. June 12, 2016 http://www.uwec.edu/CETL/resources/upload/Engaging-the-Millennial-Generation.pdf

—Joe Grimm is visiting editor in residence in the School of Journalism.

Loafers and lax rules give group work a bad reputation

"I understand the idea that group work can be very helpful in helping students work together and learn from each other, but professors need to establish clear guidelines for this."

"I'd genuinely rather write a 10,000-word essay than do horrific compulsory yet unrelated to your course group work tasks that loom over you."

"Hearing my prof say 'group work' makes me cringe bc it's usually me doing all the work."

"Would seriously ask the prof if we could remove the name of those who will not contribute anything in the group work."

"And I hate when the prof pulls the 'you'll do group work in the workforce.'"

A popular cause of venting for many college students, especially on online forums, is mandatory group work.

Although these assignments aren't always terrible experiences, many students would rather work by themselves or in pairs. Some students report greater stress and anxiety in group work than in individual assignments, where they have more control and responsibility.

Who doesn't complain about group work? Maybe the students that are being complained about.

Some reasons for the gripes:

- Students often feel like they have to put in more effort for group work than for individual assignments. While the intent is to get them to learn to work with others, they are learning less about the course content.
- Often, the students who do the work get slammed near deadline when it becomes clear that others are not doing their parts. The big take-away for students who pitch in is that they'll suffer if they have to work with students who goof off.
- Group grades make the working students feel that they are being punished while there is less accountability for group-work loafers.

- Students want clearer guidelines about how much work each group member needs to put in to receive full credit

In an article about why students hate work groups, published on Magna Publications' Teaching Professor blog, Maryellen Weimer wrote, "Many students hate group work. Why? I think there are three reasons. First, some students (like most faculty) aren't very good groupies. They don't learn well in social contexts. ... Second, students hate group work because faculty design is poor. The grade is a group grade—everybody gets the same grade. There's no individual accountability. So, if a student lets the group down, the rest of the group takes up the slack or suffers the consequences. ... Finally, students hate groups because groups make them feel vulnerable individually."

Strategies

Weimer isolates two dynamics affecting perceptions of group work: student slackers and systems that do not hold everyone accountable and punish those who work the hardest. Professors can't do much about the first problem, but they are responsible for the second.

Here are strategies for better group work:

- State clear guidelines in the syllabus about the minimum amount of work expected from each student.
- Explain the idea behind group work before you assign it.
- Use non-graded group work to warm students up to graded group work and to encourage them to mix.
- Assign group work a few weeks into the term after students know each other.
- Try not to have more than three or four people in a group, as they have more scheduling conflicts and more chances to have a loafer.
- Use evaluation sheets for all group work assignments. Some professors have group members evaluate each other. Some ask for self evaluations, compare them and even grade them.

- Be receptive to students who have problems with the group or the assignment.
- Explain the penalty for loafing.
- During extended group work assignments, check in.

Resources

Weimer, Maryellen, ed. "Effective Group Work Strategies for the College Classroom." Faculty Focus, Higher Ed Teaching Strategies from Magna Publications. June 12, 2016 http://www.facultyfocus.com/free-reports/effective-group-work-strategies-college-classroom/

Weimer, Maryellen. "Why Students Hate Work Groups." Faculty Focus, Higher Ed Teaching Strategies from Magna Publications, July 1, 2008. June 12, 2016 http://www.facultyfocus.com/articles/teaching-and-learning/why-students-hate-groups/

—*Palak Sabbineni is a communication major and public relations minor.*

There is an arms race and many shades of gray in academic fraud

"I'm sorry you thought I was plagiarizing when I turned in an assignment similar to someone else's, but it was actually a coincidence that we had the same topic … it was, in fact, a 200-person class."

"Why did I lose five points for turning in my assignment an hour late, but the guy sitting next to me faced almost no penalty for plagiarizing his paper off of the internet?"

Several studies show that plagiarism and academic fraud are rising. They are fueled by pressure to hyper-achieve in a world of points, tests, grades and scores. Technology, a great research tool, is also a source of material for the desperate. Students who have heard about copying since elementary school have also seen music and videos sampled, borrowed, sliced, diced and re-released and might not see the dangers.

There is an academic fraud arms race with new ways to cut corners and new tools to detect it. One of the new weapons is prompt.com, a website that invites students to submit their papers for grading and corrections before they submit them to their instructors. And standards vary by discipline. Phony research, mass cheating and prominent examples of plagiarism have left no field untouched. There has even been cheating on ethics exams.

Consequences can be grave for students who cheat and it takes a toll in time and emotional energy on the professors who must detect fraud to protect the reputation and integrity of their institutions.

Students are outspoken on the issue and divided. Some say the rules are unclear. Other says the pressure to cheat is too great. And some students say the punishment for peers who commit fraud is too light.

Students and instructors would be further ahead if academic fraud could be prevented, reducing the need for punishment.

Strategies

Academic integrity is, for some students, not a black and white issue, but many shades of gray. Many times the first defense is, "I just didn't know that was wrong."

Ann Hoffman, assistant dean of undergraduate education in Michigan State University's College of Communication Arts and Sciences, said professors can save themselves and their students some trouble by anticipating issues.

Crunch time: Hoffman said the most important work of the term comes at the end, when students feel the greatest pressure to cut corners. There is the stress of seeing how assignments missed earlier are weighing down grades and there's a pileup of work when everyone is trying to get things done. They have a fear of failing and the level of desperation goes up, she said.

Hoffman said the end of the academic year seems to be the worst time for fraud. Students are trying to get scholarships, internships or jobs, and perhaps registering for the next year's classes. Some will be graduating soon and wondering what to do with their lives. Pressure builds. "If sand gets dropped on a scale, eventually the scale tips," she said, and the student does something they know is wrong.

Knowing that the greatest pressure and the heaviest workload comes late, Hoffman suggested adding a mid-term reminder to the syllabus for when crunch time is coming.

Warn students about the workload ahead, refer them to academic resources if they need extra help and encourage them to come forward if they are having trouble. "Make cheating seem to be less of a reasonable option," she said.

Set limits: Hoffman said, "Students thrive better when they know what the limits are: 'If you do X, I will do Y.' They have to know where the boundaries are."

Universities and individual schools or departments typically state limits and consequences for cheating in their integrity policies or honor codes. Instructors should cite these and include them in their syllabi.

Make it specific: Hoffman said professors "need to talk about what kind of academic dishonesty or plagiarism is tied to the field of their study. They can also use language templates and online citation sources to further help students."

A recitation of the rules and instructions to read the policy aren't enough. Hoffman suggests discussion about the policy rather than a lecture.

"Address what students in your class know and don't know. Sometimes they truly don't know that the paper they submitted two semesters ago can't be resubmitted in another class for a new grade. Students are used to recycling things."

"These rules vary a little by field of study," Hoffman said. It is OK to use open-source coding for computing classes in ways that would never be allowed for content in other fields.

Citation and attribution standards vary, too. This is where templates may help. The distinction between collaboration and over-collaboration is best explained ahead of time.

"Some of it is the explanation piece. Do they get it?" she said. Integrity can be the subject of small-group exercises, discussion or quizzes. Some professors have students sign statements that they have read and understand the ethics policy, though that does not teach as well as a discussion would.

Set the example: Model the behavior you want to see, said Hoffman. "I don't know that faculty always cite where their sources are." When students see professors use material without attribution, they would be justified in wondering why they should get in trouble for doing the same thing.

Resources

Gooblar, David. "Why Students Cheat-and 3 Ways to Stop Them." Vitae, the Online Career Hub for Higher Ed., The Chronicle of Higher Education, Feb. 19, 2014. June 12, 2016 https://chroniclevitae.com/news/341-why-students-cheat-and-3-ways-to-stop-them

Lang, James M. "Cheating Lessons: Learning from Academic Dishonesty." Cambridge: Harvard University Press, 2014.

Rubinstein, Helen. "When Plagiarism Is a Plea for Help." Washington, D.C.: The Chronicle of Higher Education, March 30, 2016. June 12, 2016 http://chronicle.com/article/When-Plagiarism-Is-a-Plea-for/235884

—Palak Sabbineni is a communication major and public relations minor.

Out of bounds

Getting names right: It's personal

"I spend a lot of money to go to school here. It would be nice if a professor knew my name."

"I appreciate the fact that you asked me what I wanted to be called because my name has various pronunciations in different languages."

There are so many ways a simple and personal thing like a person's name can lead to problems. The first student quoted above felt more like a number than a person because she felt none of her professors bothered to learn her name. The second is an international student who was used to mispronunciations and questioning looks and appreciated a professor's extra effort.

Knowing names is so important to students and the classroom climate that some universities use first-name relationships as a marketing tool.

Mishandling names can lead to awkward moments.

For many students, name problems come on the first day of class. Here's a tweet with the hashtag #GrowingUpWithMyName. "Knowing the pause on roll call in school was my name. I would just start saying 'Here' before they even tried." Everyone knows what it is like to have their name mispronounced sometimes. But imagine what it is like to have it happen almost every time—and with an audience of new peers.

While some students might offer a name that they feel will be easier to remember or say, it is not OK for instructors to rename students to make it easier to call roll.

There are those times when the professor calls a student by another student's name. Somehow, the professor has made a connection. Maybe these are the only students of their race or ethnicity in the class. It seems like a little thing, but it carries big implications and it can make others in class feel uncomfortable.

One American college student reported feeling uncomfortable for Asian students when professor stumble over their names—and then turns the mistakes into jokes or ditties. It can humiliate the student and, if they are new to U.S. culture, it can be bewildering.

International names do not have universal spellings or pronunciations across cultures and societies. The student who appreciated a professor's patience in learning the pronunciation of his name is French African. Where he is from, his name has a different intonation and spelling. The student felt very good about his class after this encounter because he perceived that his professor took the time to be personal with her students.

One international student said that she can always sense when professors are about to make a funny attempt at pronouncing her name. "They never ask first but they want to act like they know already, which doesn't usually always end well."

Because names are an important aspect of our identity, acknowledgment of a person's name and its correct pronunciation can signal acceptance of that person into a new culture. Since acknowledgment leads to acceptance, many international students adopt English names to better assimilate. By doing so, they avoid the potential mispronunciation of their names and feel like they fit in. Fitting in can enhance learning.

Strategies

There are almost as many reasons why it is hard to get names right as there are students in a class. Professors have scores or hundreds of students in a term, and new ones every term. Some professors have more than a thousand students in one term. There are a lot of names to learn.

Many names have variant spellings or pronunciations. Think of Megan/Meagan/Meghan/Meeghan. Or Jeff/Geoff/Jef.

Pronunciations can be difficult, too. How many ways do people say Tania?

But learning and using student names improves teaching.

Daniel F. Chambliss, Eugene M. Tobin Distinguished Professor of Sociology at Hamilton College, wrote "the best thing I do to improve students' work in my courses is ... I will learn and use their names. It's easy, and it works. Using those names in class is uniquely powerful."

Here are some strategies:

- Read a class roster out loud before meeting the class. Note potential difficulties. If the class list has photos, try to match them with the names. Print out the pictures and bring them to class.

- Take attendance on the first day in a consistent way with each student, even the ones with seemingly easy names. Use a standard question such as, "What do you like to be called?" One professor sends out a survey before classes begin and asks students for their name preferences. One student seemed delighted when, at the first roll call, she was called by her preferred name, which was not the name on the attendance list.

- Write phonetic spellings down when you need to. When you get to a name that might be difficult, ask the student to say it, using the part of the name you feel more comfortable with. Don't joke. Don't rush. Spend a little extra time if you must to understand, but don't make a big deal. If you need to ask the student for more help, do it after class. If you make a mistake, apologize but don't make an excuse.

Many international students adopt American names to fit in. But at the same time, there are also instances where foreign students have American names. Whatever the case may be, University of Wisconsin-Eau Claire professor Phil Huelsbeck in the department of International Education, advises that professors be actively aware of these differences. He wrote, "Without an audience, ask (repeatedly if necessary) how to pronounce the international student's name and make a note of the proper pronunciation. Some international students take on an 'American name' but it is often appreciated if the instructor takes the time to learn the student's native name, as well." It can also teach classmates something.

Marian Kisch, a freelance writer in Maryland, wrote in the November/December, 2014 issue of the International Educator: "Even a short conversation after class about the student's home country can help the student feel more comfortable and can build rapport. Do your best to learn how to pronounce students' names, even if it takes a few attempts."

Dustin Carnahan, who teaches in the Michigan State University College of Communication Arts and Sciences, suggested customized rosters, which can accommodate extra columns for chosen names and pronunciations. Students should be able to tell the professor what they want to be called, "no questions asked," he said.

In many languages, vowels are pronounced quite differently from the English language. Laura Hahn at the Intensive English Institute at the University of Illinois at Urbana-Champaign wrote that not all languages treat vowels as English does. She wrote that names in many languages treat vowels in these ways:

- "A" can be pronounced like the "a" in "spa," not "man." Examples: Abdul, Lan.
- "E" can be pronounced like the "a" in "plate," not like the "ee" in "keep." Examples: Renate, José
- "I" can be pronounced like the "ee" in "keep," not like the "i" in "like." Examples: Dmitri, Samira

- "O" can be pronounced like the "o" in "most," not like the "o" in "lost." Examples: Nozomi, Kofi
- "U" can be pronounced like the "u" in "rude," not like the "u" in "cut." Examples: Umut, Srisucha

In "A Short Course in International Business Culture," Charles Mitchell wrote, "Most Chinese names have either two or three characters, each of which represents a sound. As in most of the rest of Asia, the Chinese give their surname first followed by other given names. For example, in the name, Wang Tai Hoi, Wang is the surname."

The student who felt that no professor knew her name would have been well served by a professor getting to know students and their academic and career interests.

In "Learning Student Names," posted on the National Teaching and Learning Forum, Joan Middendorf and Elizabeth Osborn at Indiana University wrote: "A professor who does not know his or her students' names may be perceived as remote and unapproachable. … In large classes, the task of learning student names can seem daunting, but even if the professor learns the names of only a portion of the class, a caring, inclusive atmosphere will be established." They gathered more than 25 strategies for learning and retaining students' names. They included name tags, tent cards, flashcard drills for the instructor, association and student introductions. There is probably something for most circumstances.

At the end of the day, it is always better to call students by the names they like. As Czech-born writer Milan Kundera wrote in his novel "Immortality," "We don't know when our name came into being or how some distant ancestor acquired it. We don't understand our name at all, we don't know its history and yet we bear it with exalted fidelity, we merge with it, we like it, we are ridiculously proud of it, as if we had thought it up ourselves in a moment of brilliant inspiration."

Resources

Chambliss, Daniel F. "Learn Your Students' Names." Inside Higher Ed, Aug. 26, 2014. June 12, 2016 https://www.insidehighered.com/views/2014/08/26/ essay-calling-faculty-members-learn-their-students-names

Huelsbeck, Phil. "Awareness Points for Educators with International Students in the Classroom." University of Wisconsin. June 12, 2016 awareness_points_for_educators_ with_international_students_in_the_classroom.pdf

Kisch, Marian. "Helping Faculty Teach International Students." NAFSA: Association of International Education, International Educator, November/December 2014.

Middendorf, Joan, and Elizabeth Osborn. "Learning Student Names." Bloomington: Indiana University, 2012. June 12, 2016 http://citl.indiana.edu/files/pdf/Lecture_Learning_Names.pdf

Mitchell, Charles. "Short Course in International Business Culture." Novato: World Trade Press, 1999.

—*Nichole Igwe is a journalism major and a public relations and French minor. Contributor Joe Grimm is visiting editor in residence in the School of Journalism.*

Profane professors: Tactical or tacky?

"Words and critiques affect students. We take them seriously, and when profanity is used, it feels like a personal attack on us."

"I think it is pretty cool when you swear in class. It makes lecture feel less scripted and you are easier to relate to."

Both comments were from the same student, but describe much different experiences.

The first quote was from a time when a professor spoke to the entire class after reviewing the first assignment, saying "don't f---ing embarrass me with this kind of work again." The student said the language shocked and discouraged him. He said it spoiled the environment and students felt contempt for the instructor.

The second quote portrays a much different experience, when the profanity wasn't personal. When it isn't directed at them, profanity can shake up and engage some students.

Michael Persinger, a neuroscientist and former psychology professor at Laurentian University in Sudbury, Ontario, used profanity in class. He asked students sign a "Statement of Understanding" on the first day. It listed vulgar words he might use in class discussions. Students were asked to acknowledge that "Dr. M. A. Persinger employs techniques intended to challenge my beliefs and to develop my skills as an independent thinker."

Persinger defended his teaching tactic as a way "to expose people to all type of different words. Silly words, complex words, emotional words, profane words. Because they influence how you make decisions and how you think." He was removed over student complaints and the statement of understanding was used in the case against him.

On ratemyprofessor.com, Persinger earned an overall quality score of 4.0 on a 5.0 scale with 79 comments, many of which were positive:

"Dr. Persinger is the best professor I've ever had. He creates a challenging environment to prepare his students for the real world. He loves teaching and all he wants in his study is enthusiasm to learn. A class with him will literally change your life."

"Most amazing, wild, crazy, raunchy, entertaining lectures you'll probably ever have in university."

"Probably the best professor I've ever had. I've never had someone make me THAT interested in the lecture."

But profanity doesn't engage every student. Some students never like it. The same comment can motivate one student, make another cry from laughter and make another want to die from embarrassment. Surely, there are few words students haven't heard by the time they get to college, so there is nothing new about them. It is all about the context.

In The Connection, published by students at Cosumnes River College in Sacramento, student Ben Levy wrote:

"... profanity doesn't fly at a good job. You won't find many business executives saying, 'our profits this quarter hella increased,' or doctors saying, 'well shit, you have cancer.'"

Levy challenged profanity as a way to pique students' interests, claiming that "while cursing grabs the attention of students at first, the shock factor soon wears off, and after a few profanity-laden lectures, students become as uninterested as they've always been."

Another professor who used profanity is Teresa Buchanan at Louisiana State University. According to The Advocate, a newspaper in Baton Rouge, Buchanan used a slang term for female genitalia to imply cowardice, told female students that boyfriends will stop helping them with homework as soon as the sex gets stale, and on occasion said "F--k, no."

Buchanan defended herself. "The occasional use of profanity is not sexual harassment. Nor is the occasional frank discussion of issues related to sexuality, particularly when done in the context of teaching specific issues related to sexuality."

She told the Huffington Post: "Good teaching often bothers students. Good teaching often upsets people. That's part of the cognitive maturation process."

Buchanan and Persinger were fired, extreme cases in the struggle between free speech and civility. For us, the issue is whether profanity improves teaching.

Strategies

There are engagement strategies that do not offend students, lose their novelty or lead to the dean's office. Here are examples of professors who have earned SAGE Teaching Innovations & Professional Development awards with advice on how to keep college students engaged. Their quotes appeared in a Sage Connection Insight series on student engagements.

Jason Freeman, a teaching fellow at the University of North Carolina at Chapel Hill, described his engagement approach in three steps that consider different types of student learners.

Freeman starts his classes by catering to auditory learners with short, 15-minute lectures. Freeman wrote "During these lectures I summarize what the students read during the previous night and provide additional context to those readings."

Then, Freeman engages visual learning through videos. He wrote, "I find these videos useful because they reinforce specific points and give a visual and/or auditory dimension to the subject matter."

Then, for those who learn more through participation, Freeman includes a small-group discussion or activity. Freeman wrote that these tactics force "students to read and think deeply about what they read," and "force students to be engaged with the class who may otherwise 'tune out' during lecture-based courses." He also wrote that they "allow students to learn from and teach each other."

The varied approach is also present in Matthew Martinez' strategy. A doctoral candidate at the University of Texas at San Antonio, Martinez wrote:

"I taught an 8:30 a.m. course and I had to keep students engaged by having a diverse set of material and good pacing. Since the course was an hour and 15 minutes, I divided it in several segments which included: a quiz over the assigned readings; an intro to the topic; 35 minutes of traditional PowerPoint lecture; and the rest of the course for in-class discussion ... By changing pace throughout the class period it allowed students to remain engaged and gave a diverse style of instruction to help students of different learning styles."

These professors recognize that people learn in different ways and that, while students have dominant learning styles, they use more than one. They planned lessons to reach all their students with a mix of techniques including active learning. In their lessons, classic educational fundamentals give lectures more punch than f-bombs can, and they alienate no one.

Resources

"18 Ways to Engage the College Classroom (Part III)." Sage Connection Insight, Aug. 20, 2015. June 12, 2016 http://connection.sagepub.com/blog/ sage-connection/2015/08/20/18-ways-to-engage-the-college- classroom-part-iii/

Crone, Ian, and Kathy MacKay. "Motivating Today's College Students." Peer Review, Association of American Colleges and Universities, 9, 2007.

Gorham, Joan, and Diane M. Christophel. "Students' Perceptions of Teacher Behaviors as Motivating and Demotivating Factors in College Classes." Communication Quarterly, 1992.

—Natalie Kozma is an advertising and public relations major.

A professor walks into a classroom: Humor 101

"I may have laughed at your sexual jokes relating to the curriculum, but it's only because it made me uncomfortable and I didn't know how else to respond."

"Your 'jokes' about certain racial groups are not funny. They perpetuate stereotypes and make me think less of you as a teacher."

Plenty of research supports the value of humor as a teaching tool. Humor can improve the atmosphere, and some researchers theorize it helps capture students' attention, which aids learning.

However, it seems to be getting harder to be funny on campus. Some jokes, even ones that once worked, can upset or offend, spoiling the lesson rather than enhancing it. It is as though the out-of-bounds line has been moved.

Comedian Jerry Seinfeld told ESPN radio host Colin Cowherd, "I don't play colleges, but I hear a lot of people tell me, 'Don't go near colleges. They're so PC.'"

The acceptability of humor is about more than where today's taste lines are drawn. There is a major distinction between being a stand-up comedian on stage and being a professor in lecture. The audience's expectations are different, and jokes don't work equally well in both venues. If a professor has to say "I was only joking," there's an issue.

Perceptions of appropriate humor vary for professors just as they vary for stand-up comedians. Comedy is completely subjective. There are comedians who keep it clean and those who make a living with sexual and racial jokes. Both make people laugh.

Peter McGraw teaches marketing and psychology at the University of Colorado-Boulder. He studies humor. He explores "Benign Violation Theory," which says that "laughter and amusement result from violations that are simultaneously seen as benign." Sometimes the root of what makes something funny is how it affronts or violates us, but in a way we understand to be harmless.

In the classroom, however, some students don't take jokes as harmless. They take offense.

Amer Zahr is an adjunct professor and a standup comic. He teaches law at the University of Detroit Mercy. He described students as more hypersensitive than older audiences. Zahr, who is Palestinian American, often pokes fun at Arab stereotypes, such as all Palestinians hate Jews, which might not sit well with certain audience members.

"Remember, art is about pointing out the absurd, especially comedy," explained Zahr. "We're pointing out how absurd the stereotype is. Sometimes people can't differentiate between using it, and making fun of it, and so it creates a hypersensitive atmosphere on campuses, which is definitely not conducive to comedy, but in a bigger way might not be conducive to debate and discussion, either."

"There are certain lines you don't cross if you are in the classroom," said Zahr. "What I do when I do my comedy is what we call 'crowd work,' so I'm picking on people, asking them their name. That would be too much in the classroom."

Melissa Wanzer, a professor in the communications studies department of Canisius College, wrote a chapter called "Use of Humor in the Classroom: The Good, the Bad and the Not-So-Funny Things That Teachers Say in the Classroom." It appears in "Communication for Teachers" by Joseph L. Chesebro and James C. McCroskey. Wanzer explained the perpetual nature of some professors' inappropriate use of comedy. She wrote that students are often afraid to challenge a professor's offensive joke because they "risk being the person that has no sense of humor." The majority of the class could be laughing, but students who are offended might remain silent rather than be the one to question the professor.

"Some professors are reinforced because students are laughing, but it is not a genuine laugh. It is an uncomfortable laugh," explained Wanzer. "As in 'boy, I'm really uncomfortable with this,' as opposed to 'wow this is really funny.'"

Typically, those reactions stem from humor that targets students on individual differences. This could be sex, race, ethnicity, sexual orientation and age. Humor that stereotypes student groups such as sororities, clubs or athletic teams can be taken personally by students who are in those groups.

According to Wanzer, jokes about specific students are almost always out of bounds, even when professors feel they have what Wanzer describes as a "green light," or a mutual understanding that it is OK. For instance, a professor might tease a student for wearing a certain clothing item or hairstyle. Wanzer still believes this is dangerous "because those other students don't know and aren't aware of that relationship you have and that might make them uncomfortable."

Strategies

Though humor has become dicier, professors should not drop it out of their teaching repertoire. When used well, it works. Some professors cannot help but use comedy in their teaching. Others might never use it.

Zahr said, "I don't think it (comedy) could lend itself to all topics. It depends. Definitely not to all professors. If you're using comedy for what it's supposed to be, which is trying to make somebody understand something while laughing—because when you make somebody laugh they're listening to you, it's very powerful."

Zahr explained how he integrates comedy into his teaching.

"I think of it quantitatively. If I'm in the classroom, it should be 90 percent academic so they know that they're learning something and maybe 10 laughter so that they just can break it up every now and then because we are talking about some deep stuff. In a comedy show it would be different, the opposite."

Wanzer recommended that professors remember that students are not expecting them to be funny. While students do not expect professors to make them laugh, they do expect professors to help them learn and remember. Wanzer offered three guidelines for professors who want to use humor as a teaching tactic.

Is it offensive? Humor that targets students on individual differences, like sex, race, ethnicity, sexual orientation and age should never be used. More universally inappropriate humor targets groups. So humor about sororities, fraternities, teams, groups or clubs that lumps people together could be taken personally, even though not intended that way.

Does it relate to the material? It is important to connect humor to the course material. Professors can use humor as a way to increase the stickiness of the material to help students recall it later. This can be a funny story, a funny example, a cartoon or a video clip.

Can students relate to it? Using jokes that students don't understand or have trouble relating to usually detracts from learning. Wanzer said students say the most important element of finding something funny is that it is relatable.

Wanzer further advises professors to use self-disparaging humor rather than target a student. She explained it is usually safe to make fun of yourself, but never acceptable to make fun of a student.

Resources

Flanagan, Caitlin. "That's Not Funny: Today's College Students Can't Seem to Take a Joke." The Atlantic, 2015.

McGraw, Peter, and Joel Warner. "The Humor Code: A Global Search for What Makes Things Funny." New York: Simon & Schuster, 2015. Print.

—Natalie Kozma is an advertising major and public relations minor. Peter McGraw photo by Lindsay Roberto, used under Creative Commons license 3.0 https://commons.wikimedia. org/w/index.php?curid=22436479

College can be a lonely place for conservatives

"I thought it was wrong when you started a political debate in class but wouldn't let anyone share their views if they opposed yours. Professors are meant to teach students how to think, not what to think, and when you share only one view in class, I feel that you are trying to manipulate our opinions."

"My professor called Republicans 'brain dead.'"

"When your teacher starts class by saying 'I'm a liberal, but I am more than open to hear everyone's opinion … '"

College is the time for students to form their own opinions, and political discussions are an important part of developing perspectives. Being exposed to a variety of views can challenge students' beliefs and help them gain a framework for thinking about and discussing issues. It is helpful to have professors who encourage discussions and allow all points of view an equal footing. However, some conservative students find campus to be an unfriendly place for their ideas. One student recalled a professor's offhanded joke about the Republican Party and its "idiot" candidates.

Comments like this can further distance conservative students who may already feel isolated from their peers. The Pew Research Center and others find that young people, and those with more college education, lean to the political left. Studies and books also say that most college faculties lean left.

One student gave a heartfelt response about a former teacher that encouraged her students to be active politically. He expressed that her openness in the classroom was one of the many traits that made her a trustworthy professor. "She was an activist and you knew it by the passion she displayed whenever an issue came up in class. I remember her encouraging students to look into protests and attempt to understand the issues these demonstrations were based from. In an active democracy, public protest is a principle tenet guaranteed by the First Amendment and in class she made sure her students were made well aware. Her teachings helped construct my current standard (for) journalists and others in the news media."

By mocking political views, professors can either provoke debate or shut it down. All things being equal, we would want more debate, but all things are not equal on campus, and conservatives who think that neither students nor professors will welcome their opinions may hold back.

In "Why Are Professors Liberal and Why Do Conservatives Care?" sociologist Neil Gross estimates that half of professors would describe themselves as being "left or liberal," making the group about three times more liberal than U.S. adults overall. He estimates that about four percent of college professors are economic conservatives and writes they tend to be concentrated in accounting, economics, management information, marketing and electrical engineering. This adds up to an environment where conservative students are more likely to be treated as outsiders, and it can happen in classes that are not about politics. One student remarked about a professor who went on a rant about gun control in a Spanish class.

The country's political and social divisiveness means that some students who identify as Republicans say that others then also label them as racist or homophobic. When that happens, a professor can step in and get such discussions back on track.

One student said that a professor explained the liberal side of an issue in detail and then said he didn't know enough about the other side to teach it. Teaching or advocating just one side leaves some students feeling they must go along to get along. Given the professor-to-student power differential, some students fear their grades might suffer if they push back.

While opposing points of view can provoke thought, when accompanied by a lack of recognition for or knowledge about the other side, it can make students reluctant to speak up, ask questions or talk to their instructors.

Strategies

In a National Public Radio report "The Political Classroom: Evidence and Ethics in Democratic Education," authors Diana E. Hess and Paula McAvoy offered some guidelines.

Hess is dean of the University of Wisconsin-Madison's School of Education. McAvoy is director of The Center for Ethics & Education in the school's Wisconsin Center for Education.

According to Hess, redirecting discussions toward open-ended questions and not making them biased or framing them from a particular ideology is key to creating an open conversation among students and professor.

Hess said, "there are classes that are more similar than they are different, and teachers have to use a lot of strategies to bring differences into the discussion. Those strategies might include bringing in guest speakers or making sure the materials the kids are using to prepare for discussion are full of multiple and competing ideas."

Bringing outside people into the classroom to give variety shows students that the teacher cares for everyone's opinion. Variety is ideal for an interesting learning environment.

One of the main goals of every classroom should be to keep the lesson plan on track. On its Teaching@CSU website, Colorado State University suggests goal-oriented discussions in which professors share the objective and can redirect the conversation if it goes off track.

The second feature of a lesson plan geared to fruitful discussion is to ask goal-oriented questions. This refers to creating questions that go in the direction of the daily lesson plan and align students with the objective so everyone stays on the same page.

Third is to avoid being derailed. In other words, don't follow irrelevant questions that could veer from the goal of the lesson plan. If the lesson begins to go off track, refer back to the original topic by using examples everyone can relate to.

Lastly, if the discussion jumps the tracks, have students submit essays with their views on the topic that got the class off topic in the first place. This allows everyone to express his or her opinion without offense or sidetracking.

Resources

Drummond, Steve. "Politics in the Classroom: How Much is Too Much?" National Public Radio, Aug. 6, 2015.

Gross, Neil. "Why Are Professors Liberal and Why Do Conservatives Care?" Cambridge: Harvard University Press, 2013.

"What It's Like to Be a Conservative on a Liberal College Campus." By Ryan Struyk. ABC News, April 25, 2014.

—Molly Jensen is an advertising major and public relations minor. Contributor Andrew DiFilippo is a packaging major.

Remarks about appearances are more than skin deep

"My math professor knows my name and without a doubt comments on my appearance every class. Today's comment was 'glammed up homeless.'"

Making a good first impression is important, and more often than not an individual's appearance is the first thing people notice. However, students come to class to learn—not to be singled out for unwelcome attention for the way they look or what they wear.

Regardless of whether a professor means well by a comment, remarking on students' appearances can create an awkward environment. Students in one class said they didn't want to attend lectures at the risk of being the professor's next target. "One of my professors always had a way of making the classroom uncomfortable to be in. He always seemed to add in personal, unsettling opinions to the class discussion, and they were always uncalled for, rude and uncomfortable. Another day he made sexist and sexual comments about women and where they stand in comparison to men. He made an inappropriate comment about my legs when I was wearing a skirt and even went as far as to say that women shouldn't be allowed to wear tops that have words written across their chest as it makes men stare at their breasts."

In 2015, Reddit's "Ask Academia" section lit up with comments when a student posted this: "I'm an undergrad taking this professor's evening course to fulfill a graduation requirement. A main component for the class is an individual research project, which requires one-on-one meetings with the instructor. So far, we've had three of these and each time he has complimented some aspect of my appearance: clothing, hairstyle, etc. On Friday, the color of my toenail polish was the subject of choice."

Studies at Metropolitan State University of Denver in 2015 revealed that among female students with similar credentials, those rated as more attractive also received higher grades than women rated as less attractive. For male students, the same study indicated no significant relationship between attractiveness and grades. The differences disappeared for online classes. Knowing this, an instructor's comments about appearance may be seen as having a relationship to grades.

Early in 2015, Rutgers Law-Camden Vice Dean Adam F. Scales addressed law students for commenting on the appearance of female professors in course evaluations. In a school-wide email he wrote: "It has come to my attention that a student submitted an evaluation that explored, in some detail, the fashion stylings of one of your professors. It will surprise no one possessing the slightest familiarity with student evaluations that this professor is a woman. Women are frequently targets of evaluative commentary that, in addition to being wildly inappropriate and adolescent, is almost never directed at men. Believe me, I am about the last person on this faculty for whom the 'sexism' label falls readily to hand, but after a lifetime of hearing these stories, I know it when I see it."

Strategies

There are two issues for the reader to consider. One is the appropriateness of teachers making remarks about students' personal appearance. Generally, the more detailed or selectively applied the remark is, the greater the chance for trouble. While a cursory remark that a student got a haircut or is wearing a suit might not cause discomfort, there seems to be scant evidence that remarking on student appearances elevates rapport or teaching effectiveness. In the absence of a benefit, why do it? Observations about appearance are unlikely to add anything and can take something away.

Instead, professors can use their platform and resources to encourage classroom discussion and uphold professionalism, as Scales did.

The other issue, as the Metropolitan State study pointed out, is the relationship of students' appearance to grading equity. There are several ways to ensure that grades are based on performance. Here are some strategies toward that end:

- Many universities have a division dedicated to assisting and training professors on diversity and inclusion. Attend on-campus workshops on diversity and inclusion and take advantage of any online tools and guides for professors.
- To ensure impartial grading, establish written course objectives and grading procedures at the start of the term and follow them throughout.
- Provide consistent progress updates to students, as evaluation is essential to the learning and teaching process.

Resources

Angel, Angelo. "Rate My Professor Ranks Professors' Skills, Appearance." Kent State University's KentWired.com, Feb. 17, 2016. June 12, 2016 http://www.kentwired.com/latest_updates/article_e3b0b45e-d5aa-11e5-b240-9b0e0c2c9bcd.html

Jaschik, Scott. "New Study Finds That Women Who Are Not Considered Attractive Receive Lower Grades." Inside Higher Ed, Jan. 5, 2016. June 12, 2016 https://www.insidehighered.com/news/2016/01/05/new-study-finds-women-who-are-not-considered-attractive-receive-lower-grade

Perlmutter, David L. "Physical Appearance and Student/Teacher Interactions." Education Digest: Essential Readings Condensed for Quick Review, March 2005. June 12, 2016 http://eric.ed.gov/?id=EJ741293

University of Tennessee-Chattanooga, Graduate and Teaching Assistant Information. "Impartial Grading." 12 June. 2016 http://www.utc.edu/walker-center-teaching-learning/orientation/graduate-teaching-assistant/impartial-grading.php

–Hannah Watts is a journalism major and public relations minor.

Technology

Email etiquette starts with good ground rules

"When you email a professor before a deadline about a problem with the system and they reply a week later with 'it's way late.'"

"I stayed up late to finish my paper, to wake up to an email from my professor saying class is canceled, paper due next week."

Email has become a vital communication tool and, when used properly, can be amazing. However, email comes with silent expectations from both parties. For email to be effective, students and professors must follow basic email etiquette.

Many students love the surprise email that class is canceled … that is, if the email comes far enough in advance. Students do not like getting an email 15 minutes before class notifying them it is canceled. By this time, some students have already forced themselves out of bed, dressed, gotten into their cars, driven to class, paid for parking, all just to be sent home. Last-minute notices and late replies can become problems.

While there are many similarities between business email etiquette and email etiquette in college, there are also some considerable differences. College email etiquette may be new for professors who began their careers in a business setting where conventions and the expectations of bosses and clients are different than students' concerns.

Regarding email, what do students want from their professors? There is a lot of formal advice online by administrators and faculty telling students how to use email, but students do not have a forum to post their own advice to professors. Instead, student advice about email shows up on Twitter:

"I get really annoyed when a professor doesn't answer an email for 5 days"

Students want timely responses.

"Professor sends an email saying class is cancelled 15 minutes before class. #annoyed"

Students want important emails, such as those regarding class cancellations, altered due dates, and different locations, far in advance. Some professors teach in the same buildings where their office is, while students might have to travel all over campus to meet teachers. It's best to send emails at least one day in advance, if not more.

"One of the most annoying things is when you type a long, thought-out email to your professor and he responds with one word."

Students are asking for thorough explanations in emails. Enough context should be provided to properly address concerns.

"I just love how my professor said she would email us the test review over break and hasn't yet."

A promise is a promise, and students will be checking their email to see that it is kept.

"When you email your professors thinking you're going to fail a project, and he emails you back with a Bible verse and hope #thankyouprof."

Strategies

While email etiquette is not exactly the same in business and in college, they do overlap. These suggestions from Business Insider work for just about everyone:

Good subject lines: A subject line tells the reader what the email will cover. An inadequate subject line could mean the receiver skips the email without reading it. Effective subject lines could include "Change in assignment due date" or "Extra credit opportunity." Simple and direct subject lines may help ensure that students open the emails.

Proper punctuation: When used properly, exclamation points can effectively add emphasis. But when over used, email messages can come across as angry, over-excited shouting. Use exclamation points sparingly to avoid miscommunication.

Easy on the jokes: Humor is difficult to transmit through written text. A line intended to be a joke could easily be interpreted the wrong way.

Proofread: This sounds obvious, but sometimes busy professors are in too much of a rush to edit themselves. This is a small but critical step when sending an email and can prevent confusion down the road.

For the college world, Purdue's OWL writing site suggests clearly communicating email expectations to students on the first day of class in a conversation or the syllabus. Other suggestions from Purdue for professors:

- Say what subjects are best for email and which are better for face-to-face meetings.
- Suggest subject lines. What subject line is most likely to get the professor's attention?
- State expected response times for both professor and students. Perhaps even propose an email contract.
- An ideal timeline for sending out emails regarding changed dates and cancelled classes.

Just as some professors list cut-off times for evening calls on their syllabi, some students would like the same courtesy on emails.

Students recognize that professors, like themselves, have lives outside the classrooms. Students also recognize that professors don't mean to have poor email etiquette. However, with good email strategies, professors can make their classes run more smoothly, teach better and save some confusion.

Resources

Giang, Vivian, and Jacquelyn Smith. "11 Email Etiquette Rules Every Professional Should Know." Business Insider, Sep. 3, 2014.

Purdue University OWL (Online Working Lab). "Email Etiquette for Professors." Purdue, June 12, 2016 https://owl.english.purdue.edu/owl/resource/710/1/

—Kelly Gooch is a communication major and public relations minor.

PowerPoint: Weapon of class destruction

"If you don't have anything to add to your PowerPoint slides, how are you qualified to teach me better than my book can?"

"It's awesome that my stats professor makes a PowerPoint with 50+ slides for every class and reads it word for word from the slide … kill me."

"Wait, are we supposed to be reading this text on the PowerPoint with the prof? because I can barely even read the heading …"

Professors who read from their PowerPoint slides can seem unprepared, uninterested or simply boring. Professors are competing against increasingly sophisticated digital presentations and distractions. Boring students through ineffective use of media is bad teaching practice and will sabotage professors' intentions. As one student put it, "if the lecture doesn't add anything to the PowerPoint, what is the point of me going to class?"

It appears that PowerPoint-aided lectures are a pretty standard teaching tool. PowerPoint presentations seem easy to put together; they can provide an easy-to-follow outline; they might be reused indefinitely and can be distributed to students. While these features of PowerPoint are all positive, the seeming ease by which PowerPoint lectures are created is not lost on students. Some students complain about professors requesting original, difficult projects while the teachers work from recycled slides.

There are two aspects of a PowerPoint lecture for a teacher to consider: its content and its design. Professors may include crucial content on their lecture slides and supplement it with discussion, but if weak design prevents students from reading the slides, the content is lost. Readability is diminished by using hard-to-read fonts such as Comic Sans, which is bound to cue eye rolls, combining similar colors for background and text, or making text too small. In contrast, a presentation that is so beautiful it appeases even the design guru in class needs the essential information to be effective. Weak content or design can kill a presentation.

If slides contain too much text to be read and understood, students may lose focus or think the professor copied the slide straight from the book. Slides that repeat the same points can seem redundant and boring. Additionally, excessive use of visuals or animated transitions can take the focus away from content.

PowerPoint is a handy program, but when misused it can destroy a lesson with boredom and confusion. While presenters may use the program to organize material they teach, it is most effective when slides supplement or reinforce what professors say, rather than repeat textbook material. Another form of unwanted repetition is reading to the class from the screen.

Content strategies

Dustin Wax, who has written frequently on the use and abuse of PowerPoint, advises "Make sure you write out or at least outline your presentation before trying to put together slides."

Wax recommends that PowerPoint contain a hook to capture attention at the beginning and that the presenter uses questions to connect the audience with the content. He also reminds presenters that they, not the slides, are presenting, and they should neither read the slides nor drone in a monotone.

Two Muhlenberg College psychology professors developed PowerPoint techniques based on Baddeley and Hitch's model of working memory and students' opinions. Professors Laura Edelman and Kathy Harring reported that students learn more from PowerPoint when instructors:

- Write short phrases rather than paragraphs.
- Talk about the information on the screen.
- Use relevant photos. Irrelevant pictures are worse than none.
- Distribute slides before class.

Similarly, Michigan State University professor emeritus Stephen Yelon suggests that, if a PowerPoint slide requires punctuation, the instructor do some "word weeding" to lessen the cognitive load of the slide.

If a professor wishes to distribute a lot of notes with the PowerPoint, that is fine, but the notes should be entered as notes and handed out as an outline and not shown on the screen.

Design strategies

Doug Lowe, author of 40 "For Dummies" books, including one on PowerPoint, has several suggestions for effective PowerPoint design. Here are five:

- Make everything 24-point type or larger.
- Use color combinations that PowerPoint suggests.
- Keep backgrounds clean.
- Limit slides to five lines. Better yet, drop the type and use a memorable image.
- Keep the number of section and elements in graphics small and make the type large.

Resources

Bartsch, Robert A., and Kristi M. Cobern. "Effectiveness of PowerPoint Presentations in Lectures." Computers & Education, p. 77-86, 2003.

Center for Teaching. "Making Better PowerPoint Presentations." Vanderbilt University Center for Teaching. 12 Jun 2016 https://cft.vanderbilt.edu/guides-sub-pages/making-better-powerpoint-presentations/

Lowe, Doug. "PowerPoint 2013 for Dummies." Hoboken: For Dummies, 2013.

Nielsen, Lisa. "10 Do's and Don'ts to Using PowerPoint to Deliver Lectures That Don't Suck." Techlearning.com, March 25, 2013. June 12, 2016 http://www.techlearning.com/default. aspx?tabid=100&entryid=5541

Wax, Dustin. "10 Tips for More Effective PowerPoint Presentations." Lifehack, June 12, 2016 http://www.lifehack. org/articles/featured/10-tips-for-more-effective-powerpoint-presentations.html

—Andrew DiFilippo is a packaging major.

Managing the demons of digital distraction

"My professor is seriously annoyed that I'm always on my phone in class, like sorry your class is a joke and I'm bored."

"I wonder if my professor knows I'm so bored that I haven't put my phone down once during this class?"

"I'm in class. My phone is much more interesting than my tax accounting professor."

Students spend about 20 percent of classroom time on their phones, according to a study by the University of Nebraska-Lincoln's Barney McCoy. His study of 675 students in 26 states was published in the Journal of Media Education. Students in class send texts, email, check social media and play games on their phones, tablets and laptops. All these distractions can add up said McCoy, an associate professor of broadcasting and journalism.

Diving into their devices is the equivalent of students silently saying their phone is more interesting than the class. Students customize technology to instantly bring them the content they want most, that is, content from or about their friends, tough competition in a professor's fight for students' attention.

Why do students do it?

Many students feel comfortable using technology in the classroom because it takes the edge off their boredom, and they don't feel it hinders their ability to learn the material. Alternatively, research shows that only 2 percent of the population can effectively multitask, and digital distraction has been tied to all kinds of problems from dangerous driving to failure to absorb material. Taking notes on a computer while simultaneously checking Buzzfeed, Facebook and Pinterest does not foster the best environment for learning. When students use their phone during class it is more than just distracting. It's downright rude.

Students are not the only ones doing this. At faculty meetings, department chairs notice that professors can be just as digitally distracted as some of their students.

But what can professors do to get students focused?

Strategies

Many professors take a hardline approach to preventing digital distraction. Brian Manata is one of several professors at Michigan State University who enforces a zero-technology policy. On the first day of class, Manata explains that technology may not be used in his classroom. Specifically, phones must be put away and notes need to be written by hand.

Manata has tried running his class both ways: with technology and without. He found that in classes where technology was not allowed, students were more engaged and successful. He said the absence of distractions fostered a better environment for group discussion. The lack of interference allows students to think theoretically and critically. He also noted research that suggested taking notes by hand was more beneficial to learning.

Manata said, "Numerous faculty members have told me that there is research to suggest that taking notes by hand is associated with better learning. I usually approach my lectures with this in mind, as I try to make slides that facilitate note taking and also raise discussion questions that my students can relate to. If they aren't distracted by tech, and the classroom climate is a comfortable one, you can usually get some good discussion going. Presumably this gets students to pay closer attention and process the material at a comparatively deeper level."

Professors who feel that students are distracted have options. There is no "killer app" or "one-size-fits-all" solution, so professors might experiment, as Manata did, to determine which cocktail of strategies works best. Here are three approaches to consider:

The zero-tolerance policy: Professors explain on the first day of class that zero technology is accepted in the classroom. Cellphones should be put away and all notes should be taken by hand. Manata's advice for professors who choose this technique is to explain the benefits to students. A zero-tolerance policy is easier to monitor, and violations can also carry grade deductions.

Allow laptops ONLY for taking notes: Many students use laptops as their primary resource for keeping class notes. In this way they use a method they're comfortable with and focus on the lecture. One major disadvantage to the laptops-for-notes strategy is that it is difficult to enforce. From the front of a classroom, a professor can see only the lid of a student's laptop. If there are teaching assistants in the room, they can enforce the notes-only part of the strategy. Professors have to trust that their students are using their computer only for notes. Some professors tell students at the start of class that they will deduct points if they catch students using their computers for non-classroom activities.

Incorporate cellphones into class activity: If you can't beat 'em, join 'em, right? Many professors are attempting to incorporate technology into their classrooms instead of banning it. Examples include texting answers to in-class questions, or texting in for attendance. Laurie Petrou, a design professor at Ryerson University in Toronto, uses Twitter to engage her students. She wrote, "Research, as light as it is in this area, shows that those who tweet about the class during class tend to do better—I guess it's kind of like taking notes. Students now tweet all the time about my class, and when they do it the official way (using my hashtag), I know about it."

A strategy could also involve all three elements, depending on what is planned for the class that day. With the right mix of strategies, professors can keep their students focused on learning, recognizing that not all students are going to like a tech ban.

Resources

Ehrlick, Steven P. "Managing Digital Distraction: A Pedagogical Approach for Dealing with Wireless Devices in the Classroom." Journal of Teaching and Education, 2014. June 12, 2016 https://www.academia.edu/11608237/MANAGING_DIGITAL_DISTRACTION_A_PEDAGOGICAL_APPROACH_FOR_DEALING_WITH_WIRELESS_DEVICES_IN_THE_CLASSROOM

McCoy, Bernard R. "Digital Distractions in the Classroom Phase II: Student Classroom Use of Digital Devices for Non-Class Related Purposes." University of Nebraska College of Journalism & Mass Communications Digital Commons, Jan. 1, 2016. June 12, 2016 http://digitalcommons.unl.edu/cgi/viewcontent.cgi?article=1091&context=journalismfacpub

Myers, S. A., Z. W. Goldman, H. Ball, H., S. T. Carton, J. Atkinson, M. F. Tindage, and A.O. Anderson. "Assessing College Student Use of Anti-Citizenship Classroom Behavior:

Types, Reasons, and Association with Learning Outcomes." Communication Teacher 29, 234-251, 2015.

—Kelly Gooch is a communication major and public relations minor.

Online classes: A love/hate relationship

"I get that you are a professional and are not a full-time teacher. But you ARE teaching a hybrid class. It is very unprofessional to not respond back to your students, but also make it impossible to find a way to reach you."

"Online classes are life savers especially when you have a full-time job. You can just fit your school work wherever you want."

"I have a love/hate relationship with online classes. I love the freedom that comes with the class, but I get so irritated with the tedious amounts of homework."

Online education has mushroomed at colleges and universities and, while it can make scheduling and participation easier, it is not necessarily less work. Students who expect to have an easier time in online classes are often surprised by the workload and, when they can't get the help they would find with an in-person class, they get discouraged.

Students have varied opinions about distance learning:

- Online courses can appeal to students who have full-time jobs. One student said, "For me, working over 40 hours and attending in-person lectures would be impossible. Online classes provide me with the flexibility and confidence in order to keep my job while still getting a degree."

- Many students find it harder to learn material and complete assignments without face-to-face contact. A study at the the University of the Potomac found that only 26 percent of students were learning better online compared to in classroom courses.

- One student reported feeling overwhelmed by the amount of work involved with an online course and wished the professor would respond more quickly when the student had questions. Feeling lost in a classroom is stressful, but students can ask the professor questions. Feeling lost in cyberspace and not being able to get hold of the professor is worse.

While online classes are meant to be remote in distance, instructors have to go to extra lengths to ensure that they are not inaccessible in terms of learning.

Strategies

Online courses have found a home in colleges to overcome the limitations of distance and class size. But it is left to professors to make online classes as effective as the best students want them to be.

Richard Rose is program chair of instructional design and technology at West Texas A&M University. He wrote in The Journal, "while online teaching offers many rewards for instructors, it takes a special set of skills and attitudes to excel at it. And these are emphatically not the same skills and attitudes that make an exceptional classroom teacher."

A large amount of human communication is nonverbal, Rose wrote, so online instructors must make an extra effort to know their students, even if they don't see their faces every day. Rose wrote, "In my online classes, I find myself constantly at risk of wildly misjudging both people and their situations."

It takes time and effort to get to know students as well as they can be known in person, but that work can make a big difference in students' perception of the course. A student never wants to feel like just a number, so when online instructors exceed their students' expectations and make a connection, that can go a long way to creating positive attitudes toward the class.

According to Ian Heywood at the 2000 World Open Learning Conference and Exhibition in Birmingham, England, "Online learning now depends more on the ability of educators and trainers to tutor and support learners online than on the technology itself."

Regardless of the online platform, there are going to be communication difficulties between teacher and students, especially in new courses or at the beginning of an established course. Professors can reduce confusion and calls with tutorials, screenshots with arrows and lists of frequently asked questions. At the beginning, questions can serve as an early warning and can lead to a correction, preventing confusion for the rest of the class. Further, early intervention can help convince students that the professor is passionate about the content, likes teaching online and has confidence the students will learn the material.

Andrea Zellner began her graduate career teaching a hybrid Ph.D. program at Michigan State University. She advises instructors to anticipate difficulties. Teaching online courses is more difficult than teaching in person. Try to incorporate synchronous opportunities. For example, using Adobe Connect or Google Hangouts to create "well-timed synchronous virtual office hours." She writes that it helps when professors tell students they can set up additional times if they need an in-person discussion.

Faculty can help students by giving them the opportunity to critique or reflect upon certain topics that are being discussed during the course. Providing a discussion board for students to discuss and respond to feedback is important for current students and can provide valuable help for improving future classes.

J.V. Boettcher, former executive director of the Corporation for Research and Educational Networking, wrote that it's important for students to have clear expectations. Provide clear communication channels and state the amount of time students should be working on the course each week. Instructions should include how often or quickly instructors will respond with grades. Students, able to drop off work at any time of the day or night, might expect feedback sooner than professors are ready to give it, so communicating intentions is likely to help.

Just like professors, students have lives outside the classroom, or beyond the computer screen, as well. They need to have a blueprint of course requirements to be organized and to balance schoolwork and social lives. Boettcher wrote, "Being clear as to how much effort and time will be required on a weekly basis keeps surprises to a minimum."

Most online classes give students the freedom to work at their own pace. Some will run with it and some will simply run aground. To help students stay on course, provide a schedule assignment with due dates or suggestions about when to complete them. After finding that students tended to put work off, one professor added a mid-course bonus for students who stayed on track. This protected some students' grades and saved them and the prof from an end-of-course logjam.

Like all classes, online classes can also require group work. Since classes don't meet physically, consider group-work spaces like Google hangout. Provide tutorials to show students how to use them.

Resources

Boettcher, J. V. "Ten Best Practices for Teaching Online." Designing for Learning, rev. 2011. June 12, 2016 http://www.designingforlearning.info/services/writing/ecoach/tenbest.html

Rose, Richard. "6 Tips for the Successful Online Teacher." The Journal, Public Sector Media Group, June 18, 2012. June 12, 2016 https://thejournal.com/articles/2012/06/18/6-must-have-skills-for-online-teachers.aspx

Zellner, Andrea. "7 Strategies to Make Your Online Teaching Better." Inside Higher Ed, Feb. 7, 2012. June 12, 2016 https://www.insidehighered.com/blogs/7-strategies-make-your-online-teaching-better

—Nicole Kazyak is a communication major with a minor in public relations. Meaghan Markey is an advertising management and public relations major.

Life stages and circumstances

There is a first for everything

"I wish professors wouldn't assign work during class that is due by midnight. As a first-generation student, my parents don't have jobs that allow for me to not work during college. I work part time to pay for my essentials. Give me a few days to submit the assignment after you assign it in class."

"I feel a pressure to major in something that will give me a good job, so I don't have to worry about finances ever again … I always worry about my professors teaching me important things that I can use in the future."

"I am like the rock star of my family, so I feel a lot of pressure to do well in school."

"First-generation college student" is not something that students have written on their foreheads, so it is hard for professors to perceive their unique differences and the obstacles they have had to overcome to be in college. Who are first-generation students?

First-generation college students are those who have no immediate family members that have obtained a degree higher than a high school diploma. According to a 2010 study by the Department of Education's National Center for Education Statistics, almost 50 percent of the college population is first-generation students.

In The Washington Post, Linda Banks-Santilli, an associate professor of education at Wheelock College wrote, "about 50 percent of all first-generation college students in the U.S. are low-income."

In "It's Tough to Trailblaze: Challenges of First-Generation College Students" published by Diverse Issues in Higher Education, Matthew Lynch described pertinent statistics. "Minority groups made up the largest demographics of students with parents that had a high school education or less, with 48.5 percent of Latino and Hispanic students and 45 percent of Black or African-American students included. The parents of students of Asian descent came in at 32 percent with a high school diploma or less, and Native Americans at 35 percent. Of students that identified themselves as Caucasian, only 28 percent were first-generation college students." Lynch is dean of the School of Education, Psychology, and Interdisciplinary Studies at Virginia Union University.

When first-generation students obtain a college degree, family dynamics are affected and consequently produce mixed emotions about the accomplishment. Banks-Santilli, herself a first-generation college student, wrote "Guilt is one of the biggest struggles first-generation college students face." She wrote that when students disrupt the family dynamic by being the first to attend college, they can experience a shift in identity. This can lead students to "develop two different identities—one for home and another for college." Students can feel like they don't belong in either place.

Often, first-generation students go to college with the goal of helping their families. Banks-Santilli wrote that, "69 percent of these students say that they want to help their families compared to 39 percent of students whose parents have earned a degree." The first student quoted here stated that she wants to find a good job so that she can support both herself and her family. As the second student stated, many families of first-generation students see themselves as a savior or delegate, and that can put a lot of pressure or even guilt on the student. They have an opportunity that the rest of their family did not, according to Banks-Santilli, so many may feel they are leaving their families behind. That is why many first-generation students work jobs to send home money, or pursue careers that will allow them to give back.

There can be a stigma attached to the label "first-generation student," so many do not talk about their circumstances. Because these students do not always seek help, professors simply might not know which students are first-generation. But there are ways to help all students that will especially benefit these academic trailblazers.

Strategies

Jasmine Lee, director of diversity programs and student engagement for James Madison College at Michigan State University, says there are simple things that every professor can do in their classes to ensure that they are helping first-generation college students succeed.

Lee urges professors to keep several key phrases in mind: "don't assume," "be mindful," "be flexible" and "extend yourself."

Don't assume: Lee says the first thing to keep in mind is that first-generation students may have "a lack of general college knowledge," because they do not have the same parental guidance as other students. It is important for professors "to be inclusive by not assuming students can get help from their parents," and by not assuming that everyone has a working knowledge of how to use the library and how to take advantage of homework help programs. There are many things that first-generation students may not have been exposed to, so "they are navigating many new spaces," Lee states. Professors can be inclusive by learning about and explaining resources and other campus services for all students. Professors might be one of the only ways some students get this information.

Be mindful: Remember that for many first-generation college students, jobs simply have to be first priority. Most first-generation college students come from families that are financially stressed, so they often have to support family members back home and plan to repay student loans. "Because work is so important, students often find themselves in the mediocre space of a 2.5 GPA because schoolwork is second," Lee says. Professors should "be mindful of the assignments they give and not over assign." This helps first-generation students, as well as other students who must work, to do well in class by allowing them to keep up with the workload. Homework is important in college, and warning students ahead of time about time-consuming assignments or offering extensions can give all students a shot at success.

Be flexible: Another problem for first-generation college students who work is that their schedules often prevent them from being able to attend office hours. Time out of class is consumed by work, so they may not be able to make scheduled times. Lee stresses the importance of offering office hours at times that work for all students.

Extend yourself: Lee says first-generation college students, "may be embarrassed about seeking help, so professors can't assume that all students will ask for help." First-generation college students may feel that everyone around them knows what they are doing, so they might feel ashamed about asking for help. Reaching out to students is a great way of helping people from all walks of life.

According to The First Generation Foundation, "Being a first-generation college student is one of the most often cited predictors of higher education failure—a status that universally leads to lesser educational outcomes." This is why the foundation's goals are, "inspiring, serving and supporting first-generation college students." These students face many obstacles as they try to change their family's histories.

Professors can help them make sure that there really is a first for everything.

Resources

Banks-Santilli, Linda. "Feet on Campus, Heart at Home: First-Generation College Students Struggle with Divided Identities." The Conversation US, June 2, 2015. June 12, 2016 https://theconversation.com/feet-on-campus-heart-at-home-first-generation-college-students-struggle-with-divided-identities-42158

Lynch, Matthew. "It's Tough to Trailblaze: Challenges of First-Generation College Students." Diverse Issues in Higher Education, January 2013. June 12, 2016. http://diverseeducation.com/article/50898/

U.S. Department of Education, National Center for Education Statistics. "Profile of Undergraduate Students: 2007-08." September 2010. June 12, 2016. http://nces.ed.gov/pubs2010/2010205.pdf

—*Erin Merlo is a comparative cultures and politics and English major and public relations minor.*

Check-ins help transfer students shake freshman feelings

"We are just thrown in and don't get half the help that students who start from day one get."

Transfer students are "more vulnerable ... and sometimes that vulnerability lasts through their college career."

The road to college graduation is not straight. The National Association for College Admission Counseling and the National Student Clearinghouse Research Center both report that about a third of today's college students end up transferring. Nearly half transfer more than once. One side effect is a rise in the average age of college students.

This shift has significant implications for the classroom. Transfer students often come with unique learning needs. They create a new kind of educational diversity. By joining a cohort that has been welcomed, oriented and which has acclimated, transfer students can feel forgotten and confused by the time they get to the classroom. Transfer students must struggle anew to develop bonds with professors and classmates while their peers may have already established relationships in previous classes. The student quoted above said, "It's really hard making relationships with peers and professors." She compared switching schools to starting college for the first time. Transfer students enter just as confused as freshmen, but typically don't have the adjustment programs to help them. There is an expectation that by your junior year you will just "get it." For many transfer students this is not the case.

Yes, universities have a responsibility to guide transfer students in their transition, and the value of an understanding professor cannot be understated. Each professor has a valuable opportunity to make a difference.

Strategies

Samantha Grabelle teaches a college adjustment course at Bryant University in Rhode Island. The university is strictly for transfer students, so no one feels that out of place, but some issues are the same all over. According to Grabelle, "There are a lot of ways to support transfer students, but it seems most important to ensure that they feel their decision was a good one, and that they have the knowledge, resources and early individualized support to reap the benefits of their new college."

The first part of the strategy is to recognize that some transfer students learn differently. They started their educational careers in a different setting and subsequently might have a different learning style than their peers. The transfer student we quoted wants professors to know that they are "more vulnerable ... and sometimes that vulnerability lasts through their college career."

A study by the Research and Practice in Assessment Journal concluded that "educationally purposeful activities" improved transfer students' success. According to the study, such activities include:

- receiving prompt written or oral feedback
- being asked to help or tutor other students
- having career discussions
- encouraging students to work harder than they thought they could to meet an instructor's standards

The main theme of these activities is to check in on transfer students and their engagement. Feedback and encouragement help all students learn, the journal says. But if transfer students have greater needs for this, professors who pay attention to each student without even knowing who transferred can be extra helpful.

Given the variety of students in a classroom, instructors can't assume that students know what is expected of them. Even though it seems juniors should just "get it," stating expectations clearly helps transfer students who might feel in some ways like students in their first year of college.

Resources

Fauria, Renee. M., and Matthew B. Fuller. "Transfer Student Success: Educationally Purposeful Activities Predictive of Undergraduate Success." Research & Practice in Assessment, 39-52, 2015.

Grabelle, Samantha. "Understanding Transfers: Unique Students with Unique Needs." Stanford University, Tomorrow's Professor Postings. June 12, 2016 https://tomprof.stanford.edu/posting/1032

Pittinsky, Matthew, and Kent Hopkins. "Underserved and Overburdened, Transfer Students Face an Uphill Battle to Earn Their Degrees." Hechinger Report, Oct. 8, 2015. June 12, 2016 http://hechingerreport.org/underserved-and-overburdened-transfer-students-face-an-uphill-battle-to-earn-their-degrees/

Steinberg, J. "College Students' Transfer Rate is About 1 in 3." New York Times, April 27, 2010. June 12, 2016 http://thechoice.blogs.nytimes.com/2010/04/27/transfer/?_r=0

—Kelly Gooch is a communication major and public relations minor.

For older students, college is a stage, not an age

"My math teacher said to an older student, 'you look like you've seen these units many times before' holy awkward."

"Awkward older student problems: when the professor uses your resume as an example of good writing ..."

Being in college after being in the workforce or starting a family can be a challenge. Older students' transitions to college can be even more difficult when differences are singled out in front of the class.

Enrollment rates for older students are increasing faster than the enrollment rate of younger students, which means the average age of college students is getting older.

NBC reported that the National Center for Education Statistics found, "Students over age 35, who accounted for 17 percent of all college and graduate students in 2009, are expected to comprise 19 percent of that total by 2020 and students aged 25 and older accounted for roughly 40 percent of all college and graduate students." Clearly, on many campuses the days are over when college students were all 18-25.

Even when recognition is positive, age is not always what older students want to be noticed for. They may want to remain anonymous in the classroom and prefer to talk about their work and business or personal experiences in private.

The range of perspectives that older college students bring varies tremendously. They likely have different motivations and expectations. Some are intimidated by the energy and college mindset of younger students. Other older students feel they have an advantage. Some older students might need to catch up on the technology, while others can run digital circles around their younger peers. The social lives and needs of older students are almost certainly different than they are for much younger students, and it is less likely the college accommodates them.

Typical college-aged students are likely to treat older students differently than members of their own cohort. It can feel unusual for older students to have classmates the age of their own children or for them to be the same age or older than the teacher.

Strategies

Deborah Davis, author of "The Adult Learner's Companion: A Guide for the Adult College Student," recommends that professors ask older students how they can help them succeed.

First, Davis suggests professors use the older college students' experience and knowledge as a foundation for preparing lectures. Content is more easily remembered when lesson plans incorporate life experiences and relevant information that pertains to the older college student as well as the rest of the class. An older college student brings real-world experience to the classroom that should be acknowledged when trying to connect with them in the classroom.

Second, Davis advises professors "Show adult learners how this class will help them attain their goals. Adult learners appreciate a class that is specifically directed toward helping them achieve their goals." Older students, who are more likely to be paying for college themselves, are more demanding consumers.

Davis writes that professors should keep course information and required textbooks realistic and related to the older college students' needs as well as those of the rest of the class. Many older college students are still in the workforce and looking for information directly related to their jobs. While a basic teaching principle is that the best lessons have clear and relevant learning objectives for everyone, older students may more closely scrutinize lesson goals than students of the typical college age. Thus, a professor adding precision and relevance to objectives will help all students. Tightening them up will help all. Davis tells professors to use examples such as exercises, metaphors and analogies to keep class information career related.

She also recommends professors maintain a respectful relationship with older college students and not undermine their credentials and experience. By giving them openings to talk about what they know and ask questions, professors create a more comfortable learning environment for the older student and, as a byproduct, richer lessons.

Davis advises professors to, "adjust your teaching speed to meet the needs of the older learner. Because adult learners learn differently than younger students, be conscious of the rate at which material is presented." The way they learn can be as different from typical students as the rate at which they learn. It should not be surprising if an older learner is faster on some metrics. Posting notes ahead of class, or slowing down for complex concepts, can help learners at any age, depending on their needs.

Thomas Lisack, an instructor at Rasmussen College in Wausau, Wisconsin, and Andrea Leppert, adjunct instructor at Rasmussen College in Aurora/Naperville, Illinois, have published tips on how professors can help older students meet their academic goals.

Lisack recommends that professors treat older students "like the adults they are." All college students are adults, of course, but older college students bring more experience and benefit from lessons focusing on examples of skills used in real life. Lisack writes, "Adult learners will be empowered as they discover they have a great deal to teach their younger classmates, and the dynamic is mutually beneficial." Lisack recommends sharing in discussions but suggests they center on skills, needs and experiences that are not age-specific.

Lisack and Leppert stress individual development. A professor could make personal growth throughout the course as a portion of the grade. Leppert says, "I compare the first speech to the last one given when I grade to determine how they are personally improving. It helps build confidence and gives tangible areas for improvement. School is hard enough… we should point out the positives." Older students should recognize the assets gained from taking the course and the value it has added to their academic accomplishments.

Older students are more likely to be time-starved than their younger counterparts, Leppert writes. "Adult students have jobs, sometimes children and tons of responsibilities, so pack every class with information and useful activities." Lab and instructional time that lets students work on assignments and ask questions during class is appreciated. Leppert also recommends being aware that an older student's schedule might not fit as well with standard office hours, or extra sessions, and that work or family emergencies might require a different attendance plan. She writes, "Build in safety nets that allow a limited number of late assignments to maintain flexibility, accountability and expectations of excellent work."

Professors might find that older students' classroom skills are less contemporary than their younger peers. Fundamental rules and etiquette like raising a hand to ask a question may not be something an older student is used to, especially if coming from a shoot-from-the-hip workplace. Older students may not be as knowledgeable when it comes to style issues such as APA or MLA writing guidelines. Lisack advises to focus on content and be understanding of style mistakes.

Lisack says, "I have found adult learners to be self-conscious, even apologetic, when it comes to being in the classroom." He also noted, "They might even exhibit some shame because they feel decades behind their classmates. The more you can break down these walls of insecurity, the better."

Lisack recommends that professors also consider the possible technology gap for older students. Assess each student's level of technology understanding based on what is required for the class. Lisack says, "While younger students may be tethered to technology, adults have longer attention spans and traditional classroom approaches appeal to them." Balancing the online and traditional classroom styles is key for all students. Lisack says, "This does not mean you can lecture to them for three hours, but you can expect the older learner to concentrate on complex material without feeling 'withdrawal' from a technology device."

The last piece of advice from Leppert is to be creative. Build a classroom atmosphere that keeps all students entertained and engaged. Teachers should accommodate confident as well as less-skilled students when doing group projects to allow for peer encouragement and mentoring. Leppert says this strategy keeps students interested, attendance high and motivation strong.

Resources

Davis, Deborah. "The Adult Learner's Companion: A Guide for the Adult College Student." Boston: Wadsworth Publishing, 2011.

Doherty, Brooks. "Teaching Strategies for Adult Learners." Faculty Focus, Higher Ed Teaching Strategies from Magna Publications, Jan. 25, 2012. June 12, 2016 http://www. facultyfocus.com/articles/effective-teaching-strategies/ tips-for-teaching-adult-students/

Holland, Kelley. "Back to School: Older Students on the Rise in College" NBC News, Aug. 28, 2014. June 12, 2016 http://www.nbcnews.com/business/business-news/ back-school-older-students-rise-college-classrooms-n191246

—*Molly Jensen is an advertising major and public relations minor.*

Helping student-parents succeed in college

"My success, or lack thereof, on your pop quizzes and the fact that I will be absent for class during my honeymoon will NOT determine my success as a teacher. Please stop treating me like

Do student parents tend to be married, or single?

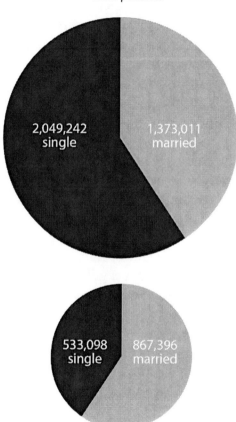

Mothers
3,422,270
total parents

2,049,242
single

1,373,011
married

533,098
single

867,396
married

Fathers
1,400,478
total parents

illustration by Matthew Hus　　　　source: Institute for Women's Policy Research , 2013

I am not good enough for you and encouraging me to change my career field. Your look of disgust infuriates me and will only drive me to prove you wrong in the future."

"When your kid is sick and the thought of contacting your professor to let her know you might miss lab makes you get sick 2."

The first quote is from a mother, wife, kindergarten teacher and one of the 4.8 million student-parents across the United States. Her days are filled with chaos and stress. Her nights are spent with books and homework. According to the Institute for Women's Policy Research, about 26 percent of today's college students have children.

The old excuse of "my dog ate my homework," has lost its eminence. As more college students become responsible for their children's educations in addition to their own, a myriad of new, perhaps more valid reasons arise for late assignments.

Consider the challenge of juggling college work, 30 hours a week of child-care and the hours needed for work. This means student parents are unlikely to graduate within six years, are less likely than other students to ever graduate at all and are more likely to be poor and have debt.

Around the developed world, studies and support groups have focused on the judgments and stigma heaped on parents of high school age, especially mothers. That shame does not magically vanish for college students. Stereotypes about being irresponsible or having skewed priorities can seem to be confirmed when students try to take care of their children's needs. However, another way to look at case of student-parents is that they are pursuing their educations in the face of difficult odds.

The prevalence of student-parents varies by the type of institution The Institute for Women's Policy Research reported that about 2.1 million student parents attend two-year institutions and make up 30 percent of the community college population. At four-year institutions they comprise 1.1 million students, or 15 percent of the student population. Just more

Average undergraduate debt one year after graduation by gender and parent status

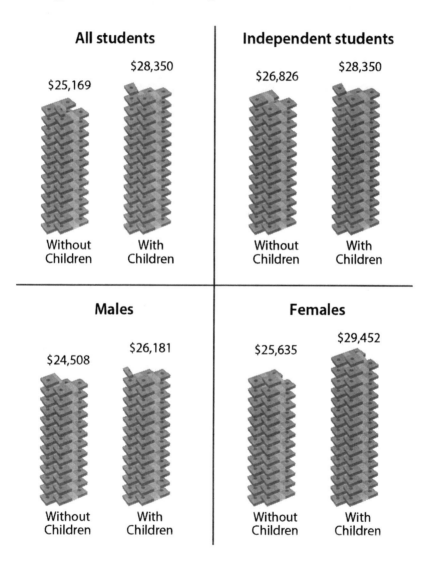

All students

$25,169 — Without Children
$28,350 — With Children

Independent students

$26,826 — Without Children
$28,350 — With Children

Males

$24,508 — Without Children
$26,181 — With Children

Females

$25,635 — Without Children
$29,452 — With Children

illustration by Matthew Hus
source: Institute for Women's Policy Research , 2013

$1,000 in debt

than half of the students at for-profit institutions, about 1.2 million, are student-parents.

To accommodate student-parents, many campuses have daycare centers, though these services are diminishing. Some student-parents are eligible for Child Care Access Means Parents in School grants. What role can professors play in helping student-parents succeed? The Institute for Women's Policy Research has some suggestions.

Strategies

- Help students who are parents by referring them to on- or off-campus child-care centers.
- Know about scholarships and grants available for student-parents. The institute found that the average student-parents is approximately $28,000 in debt. Students whose professors tell them about opportunities for scholarship and internships generally see the teachers as invested in their success.
- Make sure that class attendance policies accommodate the needs of students whose children may be sick, even though the parent are not.
- Be aware that evening or weekend assignments, work sessions and extra-credit opportunities might not be possible for students with kids. Offer alternatives.
- Help students find out whether a blend of in-person and online learning can work for them.

Perry Threlfall, who earned a Ph.D. in sociology at George Mason University as a single mom, offers these tips to instructors:

- Make provisions in the syllabus, explicitly for students with family responsibilities, regarding deadlines and attendance.
- Rethink rules about shutting off cellphones in class. Parents need to be available at all times. Phones can be set to vibrate.

- Help parents find or work with other students like themselves. This can really help with scheduling group work.
- Consider the finances of single parents. They might not buy expensive supplemental material if it means not getting something for a child.
- Ask students about their academic goals and the obstacles in attaining them.

Resources

Hopkins, Katy. "Child-Friendly College Programs for Parents." USNews & World Report, March 23, 2011. June 12, 2016 http://www.usnews.com/education/best-colleges/articles/2011/03/23/child-friendly-college-programs-for-parents

"Mothers in College Have Declining Access to On-Campus Child Care." Institute for Women's Policy Research, May 2016. June 12, 2016 http://www.iwpr.org/publications/pubs/mothers-in-college-have-declining-access-to-on-campus-child-care

Threlfall, Perry. "5 Ways Professors Can Help Me Stay in School (from a Single Mom.)" Council on Contemporary Families. "The Society Pages." Aug. 19, 2015. June 12, 2016 https://thesocietypages.org/families/2015/08/19/how-to-help-single-parents-in-school/

—Meaghan Markey is an advertising management and public relations major.

Veterans transitioning to a new theater of operation on campus

"When you have a nontraditional student who has been out in the world in one form or another, it can be slightly insulting to be treated like you're an 18-year-old kid wet behind the ears and just out of high school."

"Being a half-decade out from most other students and having had such a different experience can make it hard to relate to other students. Though we might be conspicuously different, we don't always enjoy being singled out."

"Some of us veterans have extensive experience in the field you're teaching and have valuable insight to contribute. I would appreciate for you to realize that veterans are in the room."

"I have a family and three kids at home, my family comes first and sometimes that interferes with class, but I need you to understand my priorities."

Military veterans are in college classrooms all over the country. They are not like students who have come straight to college from high school or civilian jobs. Besides differences in age and family status, there are differences in work styles, independence and security, especially in the cases of those who have seen combat.

Veterans have trained to believe that being on time is late and 15 minutes early is on time. The more easy-going atmosphere of college can be dissonant for veterans. The average student does not have the veteran's level of discipline, and that can be annoying for a veteran. Annoyance can lead to impatience with other students and with professors who do not run as tight a ship as the veteran is used to.

As a Marine veteran and a Ph.D. student in the College of Education at Michigan State University, John Christman knows how veterans experience the college classroom. He wrote: "As a former university instructor and high school teacher, I am, in some ways, in a unique position to narrow what is oftentimes a gap, or perhaps misunderstanding, between professors and students who are veterans."

Christman generally does not offer that he was in the Marines unless asked, so instructors might not know this student is also a veteran.

"The transition from the military to a university can be tricky," Christman wrote. "Not only are veterans generally a little older than the undergraduate/graduate students, but they also have different priorities and skill sets. The lack of punctuality and habits of procrastinating typically have negative consequences in the military, but I often find myself around students who do both, making it hard not only to connect, but also work with."

Besides life experiences, many veterans also have more education and work experience, yet seldom get credit for all of it. Some even take college-credit classes while in the military, but these courses do not necessarily transfer to the college transcript.

In certain cases, veterans may be required to take introductory classes in areas where they have accumulated real-world experience. One veteran reported taking a 100-level geography class that covered knowledge gained from his career in the military. He felt he had more real-world experience than the professor and thought he could have taught the class. This felt like a costly step back for a veteran. However, an overlap between a veteran's unique experience and content might encourage a positive dialogue.

Veterans of military combat may be more anxious than other students. According to the Veterans Administration, about 7 or 8 percent of the general U.S. population will experience Post-Traumatic Stress at some point. The rate for Iraq and Desert Storm combat veterans varies from 11 to 20 percent. Be aware, however, that most veterans have not served in combat and that non-veterans, too, can be set on edge by sharp noises or flashes or the feeling of being in a confined space.

Finally, veterans can do without assumptions that they are either damaged or prone to violence or instability. They get all of that.

Strategies
According to Michigan National Guard Ret. Sgt. 1st Class Nick Babcock, professors and the university should address veterans' needs as a whole.

Babcock, president of the Michigan State University Student Veterans of America, says it helps when professors get to know students personally. This is a standard teaching practice that helps all students. Babcock says this can be as simple as going around the classroom and having students say five facts about themselves that they want everyone to know. He says this helps everyone in the class understand that everyone comes from different backgrounds.

Babcock says it helps get veterans acclimated if the professor acknowledges they have advanced life experiences and understands they have lives outside the classroom.

Veterans' issues cannot, and should not, be handled solely by the professors in the classroom. The university must help as well, he said.

Babcock wants universities to have better ways to convert military credits toward degrees. Military personnel train rigorously when they enter the service and while they serve. Much of the training is in classrooms. However, military classes are not usually recognized for credit toward graduation, Babcock said. Professors cannot change this, but ought to be aware of it.

Christman wrote that students often fill in the back of a classroom or lecture hall and, "the professor then may ask for students to fill the seats in the front. I am particularly uncomfortable with this, as I do not like sitting in classrooms with students behind me. It has nothing to do with the content or being close to the professor; it makes me edgy and nervous not being able to see what is going on behind me. Additionally, I lost a significant amount of my hearing in the military and tend to position myself in a way that allows me to not only view the entire room, but to also hear well. Accordingly, I would ask that professors be aware of these situations to enhance the learning experiences of the veterans in the classroom."

As an instructor, Christman makes group work optional for his students because he knows "I do not particularly work well with students whose work ethic is significantly different than mine. I would encourage professors to take this into consideration when developing tasks for students, as veterans can quickly become impatient with students who do not have the same self-discipline."

In an article published on the American Association of University Professors website, Alisa Roost and Noah Roost wrote about how professors can help student veterans with anxiety. Alisa Roost is assistant professor of humanities at Hostos Community College in the South Bronx. Noah Roost, a clinical psychologist, specializes in the treatment of Post-Traumatic Stress and works with the Veterans Administration.

They wrote that sudden loud sounds, flashing lights or quick transitions from dark to bright can trigger anxiety. The accidental dropping of a book or snapping on the lights without warning can make class less comfortable for some veterans, other students with anxieties and students with autism. Avoiding or preventing sudden actions, or warning when a flash is imminent, can help.

Excusing students from the classroom if they are suffering from a panic attack or anxiety-related episode is helpful, too. The professor should then follow up to make sure the student is OK.

Alisa Roost and Noah Roost suggest a good starting point is for professors to ask veterans privately how they can help make classes as effective for them as possible.

Resources

Michigan State University School of Journalism. "100 Questions and Answers About Veterans: A Guide for Civilians." Canton: Read the Spirit, 2015.

Roost, Alisa, and Noah Roost. "Supporting Veterans in the Classroom." Academe, American Association of University Professors, May-June 2014. 12 Jun 2016 https://www.aaup.org/article/supporting-veterans-classroom#.V13xChWDGko

Sinski, Jennifer Blevins. "Classroom Strategies for Teaching Veterans with Post-Traumatic Stress Disorder and Traumatic Brain Injury." Journal of Postsecondary Education and Disability, 2012.

—Matthew Hus is an advertising major and public relations minor.

Commuter students in the classroom

"That moment when your professor cancels class and doesn't post anything about it and you are a commuter student."

"Absolutely hate being a commuter student when my professor decides class is going to be (just) 15 minutes."

"The commuter student struggle: Commit to the road or take that absence."

Cancelling class with little notice can be a happy surprise for the average student living on campus. For those who commute, it can become an expensive waste. Students who commute to campus face different obstacles getting to class, such as finding a parking spot or getting involved in campus life. The usual rules simply don't work for them.

Bad weather can be nasty for everyone, including professors, but for those who drive to campus, storms and icy roads present a danger. Road delays, often unexpected, can increase commuter students' travel time. No one can plan for traffic accidents or emergency repairs that result in absence or lateness to class.

In his book "Understanding and Addressing Commuter Student Needs," J. Patrick Biddix wrote that "nearly 87 percent of undergraduate students enrolled in postsecondary institutions lived off campus during the 2011-2012 academic year." Biddix lists the steps to understanding commuter students, identifying their barriers, recognizing demographics within the group and creating institutional structures to support their widely varying needs. Commuters include recent high school graduates who live with their parents and socialize with childhood friends as well as older students with families of their own. Either situation can interfere with the transition to college that on-campus students experience.

In one chapter, Ruth Darling, past president of the National Academic Advising Association, recommended "creating learning outcomes for advising commuters, using targeted academic planning techniques, and, most importantly, how to act as advocates at the institution to ensure commuters' needs are being addressed and that they found a place in the larger campus community."

Strategies

Commuter students have to go the extra mile, but a number of people say professors can meet them partway with a few accommodations.

Professors can help commuter students by giving as much notice as possible when class is going to be cancelled, so students don't use unnecessary amounts of time and gas racing to an empty classroom.

On days with hazardous weather, commuter students appreciate a flexible attendance policy or an option to take the class online. Attendance policies that anticipate the inevitability of accidents may help, too.

When adding an activity or out-of-class requirement, professors can help commuters, who may need to bring something from home, by providing notice before the day of the class. It might be just impossible for commuters to drive home, get what they need and get back in time. Complete instructions early in the term give students the notice they need to meet requirements and complete assignments.

Commuter students, like all college students, should meet at least once with their professor over the term. Flexible office hours allow students to benefit from one-on-one tutoring or advice that they can't receive anywhere else. Holding some office hours before or after class is easier on commuter students because it lets them consolidate trips. They won't have to come in several times a day, or on days when they don't have class.

Jillian Kinzie is an associate director of the National Survey of Student Engagement Institute and the Indiana University Center for Postsecondary Research. Kinzie recommends professors be in better communication with students and promote their success.

Clarify what students need to do to succeed: Students, especially commuters, will be able to manage their academic requirements if they understand all the expectations and resources at the beginning of the course. Provide examples of how previous students found success.

Set meetings: Giving students a scheduled meeting time before or after class allows them to express their issues and needs when the topic is fresh on their mind. Kinzie explains that it is crucial for professors to make time for their students because, "there is no substitute for human contact, whether face-to-face, or via email." To reach students throughout the term in case schedules change, gather student contact information, such as cellphone numbers.

Provide meaningful feedback: Constructive feedback is especially important for commuter students. When a professor is involved in a meaningful way, it connects students to campus giving students more of a chance to meet new people which, in turn, increases their satisfaction and likelihood of graduating.

Resources

Biddix, J. Patrick. "Understanding and Addressing Commuter Student Needs." San Francisco: Jossey-Bass, 2015.

Jacoby, Barbara, ed. "Involving Commuter Students in Learning: Moving from Rhetoric to Reality." San Francisco: Jossey-Bass, New Directions for Higher Education, 2000.

—*Molly Jensen is an advertising major and public relations minor.*

Getting athletes to bring their A-game to academics

"If you want to be a doctor, (and I hope you do), you are going to have to seriously assess what's more important ... softball or academics. Good luck."

"My professor just made us all clap for the athletes in the class saying 'thanks for all you do for us, you guys deserve our praise'."

"Professor basically called me a dumb jock in class tonight."

For some collegiate athletes, the association between them and their sport becomes definitive, stereotyping them as students focused only on hitting or kicking a ball or running down a field.

In 2015, Daniel Oppenheimer, a professor of psychology and marketing at UCLA, and Josh Levine, a hockey clinic manager, asked student athletes to weigh their interest in sports and academics and to do the same for teammates. Most said they care more about their studies than sports, but thought their teammates did not value academics nearly as much as they did.

The study provided a picture of how student athletes are judged, even by each other, as more an athlete than a student. One student said an instructor told her in an online discussion that she could not value both academics and athletics. The student, who said she felt she had been misjudged all term, was told to assess her values. A freshman, the student said the teacher did not answer her questions, forcing her to go to outside resources. The student said that the professor failed to give her as much help as other students received. She said she felt "worthless" or that her sport was a "waste of time."

Oppenheimer wrote that student athletes realize on their own the need to succeed academically because most know they will not become financially successful in their sport. According to an NCAA study, only 1.7 percent of college football athletes make it to the pros, although a larger proportion hope to.

Sometimes, the small number of athletes who are headed for the "big show" perpetuate the dumb-jock stereotype.

Quarterback Cardale Jones' 2013 tweet about attending Ohio State to "play football" and not "to play school" because classes were pointless had more impact than his decision in 2015 to skip the NFL draft in favor of graduating.

For most student athletes, says the NCAA, there will be no fork in the road between a sports career or another line of work. They will most likely have to pursue jobs in the field they studied. While in college, even the best athlete will have to balance class requirements with rigorous practice and game schedules. Some may also have to allot time for jobs.

Here is what a 2010 National Survey of Student Engagement learned about the average amount of time student athletes spend per week at the highest levels of collegiate competition.

Baseball	42.1 hours
Men's basketball	39.2 hours
FBS football	43.3 hours
FBC football	41.6 hours
All other men's sports	32 hours
Women's basketball	37.6 hours
All other women's sports	33.3 hours

The time crunch, in terms of hours and blocked-out hours or days for practice, can present a major conflict between student athletes and professors.

Strategies

According to Oppenheimer, professors play a crucial role in helping students navigate their way through a course. By showing concern and flexibility for demands on the student, a professor can help athletes bring their "A game" to their studies. While professors should not provide special treatment in regard to grading, validating a student athlete as a student can help develop that student.

Reminding students that other athletes also care about academics can help, too.

In an article for Inside Higher Ed, two college athletes-turned-professors offered advice on teaching the student athlete. Nate Kreuter and Eric Deiter wrote, "It should be admitted that there are athletes uninterested in or disinclined toward their student status. However, it should also be admitted that not every student-athlete has classroom anxieties. Some are superb students and superb athletes. And it should be recognized that even student-athletes who do struggle academically are overwhelmingly honest and do not engage in unethical behaviors."

Kreuter played club sports and became an assistant professor at Western Carolina University. Deiter played sports at Wabash College. Their tips are based on Deiter's work tutoring athletes and teaching them in classrooms at the University of Texas at Austin.

They offered tips for athletes who have not learned how to excel academically, but who deserve the benefit of the doubt from instructors. Their article advised:

- "Be aware of the stigmas that student-athletes face."
- "Be upfront about their dual status."
- "Work with their support structure."
- "If you're going to assume anything about them, assume that they understand what it takes to be excellent."
- "Help them transfer the mindset and skills that make them strong athletes into the classroom."
- "Respect what athletics mean to the student."
- "Try to get student-athletes to be gentle with themselves and to not overestimate the consequences of making mistakes in your class."

Resources

Kreuter, Nate, and Eric Dieter. "Teaching Student-Athletes." Inside Higher Ed, Sept. 14, 2011. June 12, 2016 https://www.insidehighered.com/advice/tyro/essay_on_what_faculty_members_should_know_about_teaching_athletes

Oppenheimer, Daniel. "UCLA Faculty Voice: Why Student Athletes Continue to Fail." UCLA Newsroom, May 11, 2015. May 15, 2016 http://newsroom.ucla.edu/stories/ucla-faculty-voice-why-student-athletes-continue-to-fail

—Kim Al-Shatel is an advertising major and public relations minor.

Health and wellness

Tips for the Americans with Disabilities Act

The federal Americans with Disabilities Act was adopted in 1990 and applies to all colleges and universities, even those that receive no federal money. It forbids discrimination in education, work, housing, communication, transportation and several other areas. The American Psychological Association has an online toolkit to help postsecondary teachers comply with the act and teach more inclusively. These guidelines can help with the chapters that follow. Some of the association's guidelines:

- Confer with the student with a disability about the most appropriate accommodation.
- Treat students with disabilities with the courtesies you would afford others.
- Respect the privacy of students with disabilities. Disability information is confidential.
- Help students follow policies such as requirements that accommodation requests be made with the disability services office. Consistency protects students, faculty and the institution. It also takes a burden off faculty members.

The association advises that instructors do not:

- Make assumptions about a student's ability to work in a particular field.

- Debate about "fairness" to nondisabled students, or whether accommodations violate the instructor's academic freedom.
- Deny accommodations or adjustments approved by the institution.

Resources

American Psychological Association. "DART Toolkit II: Legal Issues—ADA Basics." June 12, 2016 http://www.apa.org/pi/disability/dart/legal/ada-basics.aspx

U.S. Department of Labor. "Americans with Disabilities ACT." June 12, 2016 https://www.dol.gov/general/topic/disability/ada

Helping students' mental health and well-being

"I try my hardest to make it to class every day, but sometimes my depression forces me to take a day to recharge or have time for myself. Because of this, professors' strict attendance policies have made my life much harder."

"My professor knew that I have really bad anxiety, especially when it comes to public speaking. She would warn me ahead of time if I had to talk in class so I could prepare myself."

Mental health issues challenge students and professors alike. Further, mental health issues carry a stigma. Like other health issues, they are private matters, and few professors are equipped to address them. At times, however, professors discover that students are dealing with anxiety, depression, mood disorders or other challenges. Those students may need additional assistance or resources to succeed.

Some facts:

- According to Jennifer Van Pelt in the July/August 2013 issue of Social Work Today, "Additional stressors of adjusting to college life can leave some young people particularly vulnerable to developing mental health conditions."

- Research shows that most mental health disorders emerge between the ages of 14 and 24, Van Pelt writes. Furthermore, mental disorders in college-age students may increase in severity.
- Stressors such as living away from home, making new friends, a rigorous curriculum and financial responsibilities can create or worsen mental health problems.
- Stigma remains the number one reason why students refrain from accessing mental health services and supports, according to Van Pelt.

When students face mental health problems at a time that is supposed to be one of growth and opportunity, other concerns become even harder to deal with. Mental health challenges are new to many young college students, and they can be difficult to confront when the students are essentially on their own. In addition, they might not have thought about the help available on campus.

Students may not want to talk about mental or emotional issues that are hurting their classroom performance or grades. Slumping grades can compound their concerns. Anxiety, like many mental health issues, is persistent and can make even simple activities difficult. Some students may simply have trouble leaving their homes and coming to class every day.

Students with emotional difficulties may have trouble connecting to classmates, completing group projects and participating in daily discussions. One student said that even icebreakers can be nerve wracking if she feels as though she might be put on the spot or laughed at.

Anxiety and depression can manifest itself in many ways. Students spend a lot of time in classrooms, so the issues they are dealing with may come up there, or first get noticed there. The Michigan State University Counseling Center lists some signs that may indicate serious problems:

- Abrupt/radical changes in behavior, including a dramatic decrease in academic functioning
- Withdrawing from others
- Noticeable changes in mood, such as depression, apathy, or irritability
- Poor attendance
- Angry outbursts
- Difficulties with attention or memory or both
- Alcohol or drug abuse
- Marked declines in personal hygiene or appearance
- Inappropriate crying
- Bizarre statements or behavior
- Suicidal statements

Counseling center professionals said all the signs listed should be taken seriously.

Strategies

It is not a professor's role to address or treat mental health issues. However, the professor should set up an environment that is comfortable and safe. Professors may be the professionals that students interact with the most, writes Van Pelt, so they can be "one of the most important resources for identifying students who may be in distress."

According to Edward Monovich, a professor at the Massachusetts College of Art and Design, the best way to help students with mental health issues is through establishing strong relationships. It is not a professor's job to diagnose students, or to bring up their mental health at all. However, Monovich finds that meeting with his students "on an individualized basis at the beginning of semesters is a good way to establish a good rapport" early. He likes to ask his students "their personal reason for being there," and this helps him learn about his students. A strong relationship with an instructor makes it easier for students to ask for help before issues become overwhelming. Professors can support students within their limits.

When students say they have mental issues that make classes a struggle, Monovich tailors lessons individually to help them get the most out of his class. If a student expresses concern or shows alarming behavior, he offers to extend deadlines or "change assignments so that they are within their comfort zone." College is expensive, and students attend because they really want to learn. Assignments should allow them to do that, but they should not worsen students' mental health. Being compassionate and involved in a student's learning experience in class is a good way for professors to help students who may need extra help or reassurance.

Of course, there are times when students need help outside the classroom because their health or well-being is at risk. By being aware of signs like the ones listed above, professors have a better idea when to refer students to campus counseling. It is important to be aware of the different agencies that can help students. Sometimes all a student needs is the reassurance that people care, the knowledge that there are specialists on campus who can help, and the number to call.

Resources

Van Pelt, Jennifer. "College Mental Health Initiatives: Outreach to At-Risk Students." Social Work Today, July/August 2013. June 12, 2016 http://www.socialworktoday.com/archive/070813p26.shtml

—*Erin Merlo is a comparative cultures and politics and English major and public relations minor.*

Profs can help with attention and executive functioning

"I feel that your method of teaching and your style of trying to connect with the students is all wrong. By passing around a sheet on the first day showing that the average grade for your class is below a C, you made us feel like you were setting us up for failure at the start. You knew I suffered from ADHD, that I

was struggling, but you did not care. As a professor, you should make yourself available as much possible to your students. A teacher is supposed to be approachable, someone you can trust, and you were not that."

The student who wrote the note above wants his professor to know he felt like he was going to fail from the first day, just from the professor's attitude and comments. The student felt like a mere number and was discouraged.

College students can experience a whole cluster of learning challenges that include attention deficit/hyperactivity disorder and executive functioning issues. These are neurobiological conditions that have a wide variety of symptoms. They include "zoning out," distraction, forgetfulness, impulsiveness, speaking out or having trouble communicating and listening.

Neurobiological conditions affect adults as well as children in school and out. Students with ADHD have been shown to have more difficulty maintaining friendships and connecting with other students in class. Outside of class, neurobiological issues can mean social miscues and emotional instability, which can also disrupt success in college.

Dr. Stephanie Sarkis is a mental health counselor who specializes in the treatment of ADD/ADHD. She is on the staff of Clinical Research Studies at Florida Atlantic University's Schmidt College of Medicine and has written four books. She wrote that students with ADHD say things like, "I sit and read, but I get to the end of the page and have no idea what I just read."

Libby Fairhurst, author and researcher at the Florida State Adult Learning Evaluation Center, wrote that "Individuals with ADHD have a difficult time reading, focusing and staying attentive. They tend not to like reading books. They can't remember things. They get bored easily."

One student reported trouble even getting out of bed in the morning on some days.

The question is: What can professors do to help such students succeed?

Strategies

Professors are not counselors, but all can connect with students. They may simply call students by name or reassure them that it is OK to ask questions. Any student who feels an instructor doesn't care has a harder time learning the material. This is especially true for someone who suffers from neurological disorders. Students need to be reassured that, although the course is challenging, the instructor believes the students can succeed and will help.

One student said that making lectures more interactive would not only keep the attention of someone who has ADHD, but would make the lecture enjoyable for the class as a whole. Everyone loves professors who show that they care about what the students are learning and who teach with enthusiasm.

Though ADHD is a personal matter, support from the instructor helps. Even without training or knowing which students have ADHD, professors can do a lot to assist such students. Subtle signs of support can help.

Mohawk Valley Community College advises instructors to ask themselves questions like "Do you have very clear expectations for all tasks written into the syllabus," or "Are you 'checking in' to make sure the student is not struggling with the curriculum?" If a student asks for help, take the request seriously.

The College of Applied Health Sciences at the University of Illinois at Urbana-Champaign has published several instructional strategies for working with students who have ADHD. They include:

- Provide reviews or study sheets for exams.
- Minimize distractions during exams.
- Keep instructions concise and repeat them without paraphrasing.
- Present content in both visual and auditory modes.

- Break down big assignments and set deadlines for components rather than one due date for the entire assignment.
- When relevant, help choose or narrow down topics.
- Ask privately what accommodations can help the student learn and succeed.

Resources

Mohawk Valley Community College. "Faculty Tip Sheet for Working with Students with ADHD." June 12, 2016 http://www.mvcc.edu/disability-services/ info-about-working-with-adhd

University of Illinois at Urbana-Champaign College of Applied Health Sciences, Disability Resources & Educational Services. "Attention-Deficit/Hyperactivity Disorder (ADHD)." June 12, 2016 http://disability.illinois.edu/instructor-information/disability-specific-instructional-strategies/ attention-deficithyperactivity

—Nicole Kazyak is a communication major and public relations minor.

Autism spectrum issues vary but can be helped

"Wow, this professor really put an autistic boy on the spot for doing an assignment wrong."

"#actuallyautistic problems: when you finally told your professor you're autistic, but now you're not sure if it was a good decision."

"Excuse me professor, can you not use the word 'him' because I'm autistic and trans. And it causes me to have panic attacks."

Students with autism spectrum disorders, although intelligent enough to be in college, can have a tough time there. They might have trouble processing thoughts and communicating ideas. Their limited interests and repetitive behavior patterns can be an obstacle to making friends. If a student with autism is living independently for the first time, that can be a challenge, too. Changes in daily routine and surroundings can be disruptive, and certain stimuli may be distracting.

Students with autism spectrum disorders can feel excluded by teaching methods that do not fit their learning needs. Challenges include:

- Difficulty understanding instructions, especially when they are hasty or vague
- Distractions from images or flickering lights or projectors
- Lack of structure
- Lack of examples that show how concepts are generalized
- Deadlines

Strategies

Here are some ideas for creating better learning environments for all students, including those with autism spectrum disorders:

- Course structure is very important. Syllabi should be as organized and detailed as possible and they should be followed. Resist changing mid-course, but if that is impossible, notify students of changes in deadlines and assignments. In creating lesson plans, maintain a similar structure and provide an overview of topics to be covered at the start of each class.
- Give straightforward instructions and clearly convey each portion of the assignment.
- Provide multiple examples to ensure generalization of the principle.
- When verbal communication is a major aspect of a student's grade, offer exam alternatives such as writing about ideas that others expressed during discussions.
- Many autistic students benefit more from visual learning, so it may be helpful to incorporate visuals into lectures.

Teaching with visuals can reinforce lessons for all students.

- Minimize visual distractions in lessons such as flickering lights and let the student sit away from those possible distractions.
- If there is group work, support the student and stay in touch with the group to ensure everything runs smoothly.
- Students on the autism spectrum might have problems asking for help, so talk with students early in the term to develop relationships in which students are more comfortable asking questions.
- Time management can be difficult for students with autism spectrum disorders, so extended time for testing may be needed. Often, universities will have alternate locations where students can take their exams free of time constraints and distractions.

Resources

DeOrnellas, Kathy. "Teaching College Students with Autism Spectrum Disorders." Faculty Focus, Higher Ed Teaching Strategies from Magna Publications. April 17, 2015. June 12, 2016 http://www.facultyfocus. com/articles/effective-classroom-management/ teaching-college-students-with-autism-spectrum-disorders/

Morena, Susan, and Carol O'Neal. "Tips for Teaching High-Functioning People with Autism." Indiana Resource Center for Autism, 2000. June 12, 2016 https://www.iidc.indiana.edu/pages/ Tips-for-Teaching-High-Functioning-People-with-Autism

University of Massachusetts Dartmouth Center for Access and Success. "Resources for Educators and How to Teach Students on the Autism Spectrum," (2015). June 12, 2016

http://www.umassd.edu/dss/resources/facultystaff/
howtoteachandaccommodate/howtoteachautismspectrum/

—*Eric Straughn is an international relations major and public relations minor.*

Food allergies, an overlooked health hazard

"If you bring food/treats for the class, you're already winning. Just please don't forget about your students with food allergies."

"So based on what my professor said, and what's qualified as special needs that affect learning are food allergies ... I guess I'm special needs."

"Explaining food allergies and their adverse effects to your professor in lieu of missing class NEVER goes well. Just to let everyone know."

Food allergies are common and increasing. As many as 15 million Americans have food allergies, and research shows that teenagers and young adults are at the highest risk for fatal food-induced anaphylaxis. According to a 2013 report by the Centers for Disease Control and Prevention, food allergies among children increased approximately 50 percent between 1997 and 2011.

Though the larger concerns are in food services and dining facilities around campus, allergies can become a classroom issue, too.

"My university decided I was a liability, so I was essentially kicked out of school," one student wrote on her blog.

Her allergy to peanuts is so severe that her school considered it a disability. It prevented her from attending classes, group meetings, using library resources and study spots. She worked with the university's Disability Support Services to acquire reasonable accommodations for her allergy, including "peanut-free" signs on classroom doors and quarterly allergy reminder emails sent to her classmates.

Halfway through college, she alleges, she was forced to give up her pursuit of her academic dreams because she was deemed a liability. She claims her university cut off her access to Disability Support Services and reversed existing allergy accommodation policies.

Even in non-life-threatening cases, allergies can diminish student class attendance and performance, making it a concern for instructors. An allergy can be a performance obstacle that is not visibly apparent.

Strategies

- Students who hide allergies because of feelings of insecurity can have dangerous and potentially fatal consequences. Instructors should encourage students to alert them about food allergies they may have.

- The section of the syllabus dealing with accommodations should ask students to mention allergies. Will it be a problem if someone brings an allergen into the classroom?

- If certain foods are dangerous for students in the class, set policies. This can be part of first-week orientation and it can be done without singling out anyone. Medical issues should be handled in confidence, even if they affect the entire group.

- When exposed to an allergen, some people must give themselves an injection of epinephrine, typically with an EpiPen. These individuals usually carry one and know how to administer the shot themselves. Others take an antihistamine such as Benadryl. Similar responses may be required when a student's blood-sugar drops to a dangerous level. Most college students with such symptoms will know how to handle their own care. Professors should not administer medicine or treatment, but might need to call 911. An injection of epinephrine, for example, is often followed by a trip to the emergency room for observation and testing.

- Ask the appropriate university department if there is anything else that should be done in case of an episode or to accommodate attendance and performance difficulties.

Resources

Dallas, Mary Elizabeth. "Coping with Severe Allergies on Campus." Everyday Health, updated 2014. June 12, 2016 http://www.everydayhealth.com/hs/ anaphylaxis-severe-allergy-guide/ coping-with-severe-allergies-on-campus/

F.A.R.E. (Food Allergy Research and Education) "Pilot Guidelines for Managing Food Allergies in Higher Education." June 12, 2016 http://www.foodallergy.org/file/college-pilot-guidelines.pdf

—*Hannah Watts is a journalism major and public relations minor.*

How instructors support visually impaired students

"And all hell breaks loose, because I'm (sitting) in this exam crying all over my lecturer, not my finest moment, and how will I ever even pass this semester?"

"One of our teachers learned braille so that she could teach her blind student. Amazing."

"Something is broken within our education system if you don't fit the idea of the norm you can easily fall through the cracks."

Visual impairments vary widely in degree and effect. Legal blindness means that vision can be corrected to no better than 20/200. This means someone sees something at 20 feet that fully sighted people see at 200 feet. Visual impairment is defined as 20/70. Legal blindness can also mean that peripheral vision does not go beyond 20 degrees.

Many students who are legally blind can partially see, but might use adaptive devices to read, or a guide animal to help them get to class.

Many professors have neither training nor experience teaching students with visual limitations and, when a visually impaired student enrolls in their classes, they must learn quickly what to be aware of and how to make accommodations. Caught unprepared, some instructors have passed out papers to students who cannot read them, or put up slides the students cannot see. Instructors have inappropriately petted working service animals, or worried that they will confuse names of the student and the dog.

One student was unable to complete exams because, though she had met with a disability adviser in advance of the course, she still had not completed disability processing before finishing the the coursework and exams. The student was driven to tears because of the struggle she had just to take an exam in a class. Such stress can compound the feeling of being left out of lessons and material.

Many professors accommodate students' visual disabilities well. One student recalls being in a class where the instructor learned braille so she could teach better. Federal law and good teaching practice require that all students should be served, and many colleges and universities have resource people in disability offices to help by applying relevant expertise and accessing specialized devices. The challenge is that the student might be responsible for connecting the disabilities office to the professor. Accommodations are more successful for students if professors also become part of that bridge.

Strategies

Professors can do a lot for visually impaired students, even their first such learner. The first step is to acknowledge the student's limitations and get to know the person. Ask about the student's needs. According to the American Federation for the Blind's text called "When You Have a Visually Impaired Student in Your Classroom: A Guide for Teachers," it's important to know that visually impaired students are more like other students than not.

The Texas School for the Blind and Visually Impaired suggests that professors encourage students to sit near the front of the classroom so that they can hear instructions clearly. Reducing noisy distractions can help. The school also suggests that professors respect students' independence and practice patience.

Some professors have reservations about students taping their lectures to protect their intellectual property, but recordings can be a substantial help to visually impaired students. According to the Allegheny College Student Disabilities Services, recording helps students take lecture notes and play them back later. According to this office, professors who face the class when speaking, even if they have good volume, won't have their voices muffled.

Service animals, usually dogs and sometimes small horses, can distract other students. But the animals are working, and are not there for play. The Allegheny College Student Disabilities office advises that animals not be petted or addressed without the owner's permission. Many service animals wear signs reminding people that they are working dogs and should not be touched. According to Allegheny's guidelines, a harness generally means that the animal is at work.

More advice from Alleghany on communication:

- Speak directly to the student and address them by name. Just looking at them is not enough.
- Refer to others who are present or in the conversation by name.
- Speak at a normal level. Visually impaired students typically do not need more volume.
- Professors might need to amend their usual rules about not touching students to guide them into a seat or down the hall. Many students will show instructors how they like to be guided by placing a hand on a shoulder or reaching toward a chair. An instructor can then guide the student's hand.
- Don't be uptight about making a mistake and saying words like "see" or "look." Visually impaired students say

them, too, as in, "See you later." Some have good senses of humor, just like other students.

All college students share basic goals about learning, achieving and getting ready for life after college. Blind and visually impaired students face different challenges, but the more one-on-one help that they receive from professors, the more successful they will be.

Resources

Allegheny College Student Disability Services. "Students Who Are Blind or Have a Visual Impairment." Allegheny College, 2016. June 12, 2016 http://sites.allegheny.edu/disabilityservices/students-who-are-blind-or-have-a-visual-impairment/

Burgstahler, Sheryl. "Universal Design of Instruction (UDI): Definition, Principles, Guidelines, and Examples." Seattle: University of Washington. June 12, 2016 http://www.washington.edu/doit/universal-design-instruction-udi-definition-principles-guidelines-and-examples

Spungin, Susan Jay, and Donna McNear. "When You Have a Visually Impaired Student in Your Classroom: A Guide for Teachers." New York: American Federation for the Blind, 2002.

Texas School for the Blind and Visually Impaired. "Classroom Strategies for Regular Education Teachers Who Have Students with Visual Impairments." June 12, 2016 http://www.tsbvi.edu/instructional-resources/1911-classroom-strategies-for-regular-education-teachers-who-have-students-with-visual-impairments

—Matthew Hus is an advertising major and public relations minor.

For hard-of-hearing students,
simple changes make learning easier

"As a student that is hard of hearing, it is difficult to hear questions asked by students in lecture, so I really appreciate it when you repeat questions to the class."

"When the American Sign Language interpreter doesn't show up & your professor says it's OK we can still meet because you have good speech!!"

According to the U.S. Department of Education, approximately 10 percent of Americans have some hearing difficulty. Thus, instructors are likely to have a student who is hard of hearing in class at some point. It is obvious that deafness may be an obstacle to learning, but professors might not even know when a student is struggling to hear.

The range of hearing impairments and coping strategies make it important not to generalize about students. Severity varies and there are a number of adaptive technologies and even a debate about whether to rely on lip reading or American Sign Language.

Hard-of-hearing people who communicate verbally rather than with sign language are called "oral." Virginia Martz, an adviser at Michigan State University's Resource Center for Persons with Disabilities, said most students who are hard of hearing have no issues with their speech, but some cannot control their tone or volume. Martz, who specializes with students who are deaf or hard of hearing, said it is quite rare for an individual to be entirely deaf. Most individuals who are hard of hearing can hear some things. She advises professors to refrain from asking students how much they can hear. It is impossible for a student who is hard of hearing to quantify how much they can hear. Trying to answer that question may make them feel uncomfortable.

Deaf students use many types of adaptive technologies. One is Communication Access Realtime Translation. It involves a stenographer transcribing lectures as they occur so students can read them. Another technology uses an FM transmitter. In 2015 at Memorial University in Newfoundland, a professor refused to wear the device for a student who requested it. It was at least the third time she was reported to have refused a student request, citing religious reasons.

Strategies

Gallaudet University in Washington, D.C., was founded in 1864 as a grammar school for blind and deaf children. It became the first school in the world for deaf and hard-of-hearing students. It is the world's only post-secondary school in which all programs and services are designed with these needs in mind, so staff members are well practiced in using techniques for teaching the hard-of-hearing community.

Gallaudet's website advises, "use the term 'people who are deaf and hard of hearing' instead of 'hearing impaired' or 'hearing loss.' Do not use the term 'disabled' when referring to a deaf or hard-of-hearing person." Not everyone who is hard of hearing reads lips, according to Gallaudet.

Martz said only a third of the English language can be signed, so if a student has an interpreter, it can be helpful for professors to pause in their lectures to ensure accuracy of the signs. Gallaudet advises lecturers to make eye contact with the student rather than the interpreter.

Professors who are requested to do so, or who have to reach large audiences, should use amplification, Martz said. Even if professors feel their voice is loud enough for students to hear, it may not be. We have all been in situations where the speaker prefers not to use the sound system but cannot be heard well at the back of the room. She said instructors should use their normal tone of voice when talking to hard-of-hearing students, because yelling can distort speech and it can make lip-reading more difficult.

Ferris State University's Disabilities Services office advises professors in large lecture halls to repeat student questions or comments, which typically are not amplified and might be coming from all over the hall.

The office recommends professors have a section in the syllabus about accommodations for students with disabilities such as hearing impairments. The syllabus should invite hard-of-hearing students to inform the professor so accommodations can be made.

For events such as cancellations or changes in exam times and due dates, Allegheny College's Student Disability Services suggests that professors provide handouts with the information or put the information on the board or mention it in a class presentation.

Lectures are more effective if they are straightforward and well organized, whether the student reads lips or uses interpreters. Organization helps all students. Audio material can exclude students with hearing difficulties, but that is remedied with transcripts or subtitles. Whether a student can see a professor's face can make a vast difference for students who are hard of hearing. Don't stand in front of or near bright windows or screens. That can make the lecturer's face difficult to see. Once again, this is a practice that can improve communication for all students.

Arranging the seats in a classroom so that students can see each other can also help hard-of-hearing students who lip-read, and can increase engagement generally.

Finally, professors can include hard-of-hearing students in conversations, bringing them in with a visual cue, calling them by name, or recognizing when they raise their hand. It is just not right to skip them.

Resources

DeafTEC: Technological Education Center for Deaf and Hard-of-Hearing Students. "Hard-of-Hearing Students" (with videos). Rochester Institute of Technology. June 12, 2016 https://www.deaftec.org/classact/challenges/communication/hoh-students

Ferris State University Disabilities Services. "Teaching Strategies for Hearing Impaired Students." June 12, 2016 http://www.ferris.edu/htmls/colleges/university/disability/faculty-staff/classroom-issues/hearing/hearing-strategy.htm

Szymanski, Christen, Lori Lutz, Cheryl Shahan, and Nicholas Gala. "Critical Needs of Students Who Are Deaf or Hard of Hearing: A Public Input Summary." Gallaudet University Laurent Clerc National Deaf Education Center. June 12, 2016 www.gallaudet.edu/documents/Clerc/PublicInputSummary.pdf

—Eric Straughn is an international relations major and public relations minor.

You can't always see something is wrong just by looking

"I was extremely lucky to have that professor with me that day. I have thought back on that multiple times wondering what would have happened if I had left class and fallen in the parking lot or if I had been alone in my dorm. I'm lucky to have made a lifelong friend with my professor."

"I wanted to tell you if you work with me, I will work just as hard and probably harder than all the other students. Yes, I might need an extension, miss class or have to leave early. Here's the thing, though, if you give me a chance, I'll get in all my assignments. And if you give me the time I need, I'll give you high-quality work. I'll talk to my classmates, get a copy of their notes and shoot you an email if I have a question. If you are begrudging when I use accommodations, I'll do my best not to use them. But if I don't use my accommodations because you made me feel bad about needing them, everyone will suffer … Just work with me, and I may surprise you."

There are many serious but invisible chronic conditions including sickle cell, lupus, Lyme disease, depression, cancer, heart and lung disease and chronic fatigue. Although they vary, each could unexpectedly interfere with daily activities. For students with chronic illnesses, there can be good days and bad days, or even good hours and bad ones.

At the 2010 Annual North Carolina Lupus Summit, award-winning writer, blogger, speaker and lupus patient advocate Christine Miserandino told how she explained her lupus to her best friend by using spoons. She gave her friend 12 spoons to spend. These were spent to get out of bed in the morning, choose the clothes she could physically put on that day, showering and washing her hair, make food so she could take medication that enabled her to do the little tasks throughout the day, run errands and make dinner while nauseated. By the end of the day, depending on how she used her resources, her friend could end up with no spoons or even need to borrow some from the next day. But even catching a cold could prove dangerous to someone with Miserandino's condition.

Younger people are often assumed to be healthy, but diseases and disabilities do not discriminate based on age. In the United States, 96 percent of people with chronic medical conditions show no visible signs of their illness and 10 percent experience symptoms that are considered disabling. Disabilities caused by chronic illnesses can make it difficult for a person to walk, speak, eat, sit, hear or complete chores without assistance. Educators cannot often tell if a student in class has a chronic illness. Many do not report their condition because they do not want to be stigmatized, or they want to manage their conditions without help.

While a sophomore at New York University, Lily Altavena had her first flare-up of Crohn's disease. She was diagnosed with Crohn's in high school. "Having a chronic illness in college is tough. I didn't factor it into my college decision. I traveled far from home, because I knew NYU would serve me best," Altavena wrote for The New York Times' college blog The Choice. "If I got sick, I thought, I would find a doctor and get better. Easier said than done." Never thinking that Crohn's would interrupt her life at school, Altavena spent time between class, in bed, and having doctor's visits. Flare-ups caused her to lose 15 pounds in two weeks. She became malnourished and consequently too fatigued and anemic to carry out her obligations. While working an internship at a prestigious magazine in the middle of that summer, she had to be hospitalized. She needed her internship for college credit, but was forced to travel 2,000 miles home instead to recuperate. She had to take an incomplete for her internship.

Strategies

Caleb Sandoval, a chronic health and disability specialist with Michigan State University's Resource Center for Persons with Disabilities, said "Since most students with chronic health disabilities look 'normal,' on occasion, less enlightened professors will see their absences or lack of active participation in class as laziness, and the explanations that they offer for absences as less than honest."

While most students can get through a day, week, month, or a term without much difficulty, a struggle-free time period is a gift for students with chronic illnesses. Unexpected and debilitating symptoms can be exacerbated when professors misunderstand or mischaracterize them, Sandoval said. What professors don't always see is that the students are solid and they and their families have attempted to find a treatment regimen that will produce the greatest benefit with the fewest symptoms. "All of this effort is being made behind the scenes of, and in addition to, these students' class obligations and exams," Sandoval said.

Students who need accommodations are not always aware of campus services. Professors can help by directing students who ask for help to the appropriate resource center. Students often view their conditions "as illnesses and not anything that 'disables' them," Sandoval said. "So, some reluctance to registering through our office and making a formal declaration, even if it's just to us, that 'yes, I have a disability,' is completely understandable." But to receive accommodations, students may have to register. "Professors should not, however, even if well-intentioned, interject themselves without being prompted," he added. "For instance, if a professor feels that she or he observes a student with need for accommodation due to a disability, she or he should not approach this student and address this situation unsolicited."

Once a student has been assessed and reasonable accommodations granted, their validity is not up for debate. "Therefore, conversations that begin like, 'You look fine. Why do you need those accommodations?' are wholly inappropriate," Sandoval said. "Students have no obligation to defend the disabling qualities of their conditions to their professors. Their private medical information is theirs solely to disclose."

"Have the knowledge to know what you don't know, but at the same time, have faith in the university's verification system," Sandoval said. "We do our best to corroborate and verify so that professors can be assured that if a student comes before them with (documentation), there is something legit going on."

Resources

Elizabeth, Joan. "To My College Professor, From Your Student with a Chronic Illness." The Mighty, Nov. 22, 2015. June 12, 2016 https://themighty.com/2015/11/to-my-college-professor-from-your-student-with-a-chronic-illness/

Hayden, Kate, Steffi Lee, Megan Quick, and Ben Rodgers. "College Students Battle Hidden Illnesses." The Des Moines Register, April 25, 2015. June 12, 2016 http://www.desmoinesregister.com/story/news/education/2015/04/25/hidden-illnesses-iowa-colleges/26376269/

—Michelle Armstead is a journalism major with a specialization in business reporting and an economics major.

Unreported disabilities: How to help while respecting privacy

"It's very difficult when I'm trying to understand what you're teaching, but you talk as if we already know what we're supposed to be learning. Sometimes I lose motivation and confidence to continue schooling because in some situations I feel slower than the other students who seem to be following along just fine."

"I sat in your class listening to you talk about your 'star pupil,' how she gets everything right and how she is so concentrated and motivated on top of being a mother of six, so no student should ever have an excuse for slipping up. 'If she can do it, you can too.' But that's her. Everyone works differently. You don't know how hard it is for students with mental disabilities to even learn a simple concept, let alone do all of the things your 'star pupil' does."

"It's extremely hard when professors don't know what I'm dealing with inside my head, but the chance of them stereotyping me or acting like I'm broken is too much of a risk I'm willing to take."

Stereotypes influence people to hide their conditions. According to the Scattergood Foundation, stereotypes surround people with mental or physical illnesses. Stereotypes include being incompetent, dangerous and unpredictable. The foundation "seeks opportunities for productive dialogue and learning within the behavioral health field."

According to CBS News, about 15 percent of people worldwide have a physical or mental disability such as depression, bipolar disorder, ADHD, deafness or blindness. But not all disabilities are apparent, and many people choose to keep their condition a secret for fear of what people will think about them. Some students choose not to tell professors or teaching assistants about their condition to avoid stigma and assumptions about their performance.

One student said he hid his ADHD from professors because he assumed they would think it was an excuse rather than an actual reason, or that they would think he was lying to get special treatment. Another said she did not want her professors to think differently of her, as if she was "broken or messed up," or look at her every day as "the girl with anxiety" as if she were less than her classmates. Students have the right to disclose their conditions to a university office for disabilities or accommodations and then to disclose what they wish to professors only on a case-by-case basis. They can also disclose partway through the term, after they trust the instructor or find that they simply must.

A student said, "Professors should already be aware that these disabilities are real and they're out there. They should know that it is a sensitive topic for people to talk about, especially with a professor whom they most likely do not know personally. If they see someone struggling with something, they should never put them down for it."

Because students may have good reasons for not disclosing serious problems, instructors cannot accurately assume that students either do or do not have a condition unless the student discloses, and they have to be open to disclosures partway through the term.

Strategies

A syllabus statement about disability resources on campus can help students and sends a signal that the professor is approachable. Resource centers, said Michigan State University disability specialist and academic coach Shani Feyen, offer templates for "faculty to welcome accommodations and make their welcome of accommodations apparent on their syllabus."

Feyen recommends "faculty verbally discussing their openness to varied learning experiences by students. If students feel their faculty are more accommodating, or if faculty invite student engagement around the accommodations process, they are more likely to use their accommodations, which may be critical to accessing the course. An invite to office hours can go a long way." Professors who show they care about their students' well-being and success without judging might get a good idea of how to reach them.

The disabilities office at Butte College reminds instructors to "make note of the student's behaviors in relation to your class that you believe are impacting/may impact the student's learning. THESE are the focus of your interactions with the student, NOT any suspected disability." Behavioral examples are, "not participating in group work, written work much less cohesive and developed than spoken ideas, difficulty staying focused on in-class tasks, quiz/test scores not reflecting quality of work in other areas, challenges with social skills/interaction."

DO-IT, a University of Washington program, promotes success for people with disabilities. According to its website, "students are in school to learn and instructors share this goal. The field of universal design can provide a starting point for developing a framework for instruction." Universal design develops a product, such as course material, with the principle that the end product can be used by everyone, no matter who they are or what condition they have. An article in Inside Higher Ed suggested that "rather than a professor approaching the disabilities services office every time he or she needs, say, a textbook converted to digital, campus staff should work to make sure everything is accessible to everyone."

Resources

Burgstahler, Sheryl. "Invisible Disabilities and Postsecondary Education." University of Washington. June 12, 2016 http://www.washington.edu/doit/invisible-disabilities-and-postsecondary-education

Grasgreen, Allie. "Students with Disabilities Frustrated with Ignorance and Lack of Services." Inside Higher Ed, April 2, 2014. June 12, 2016 https://www.insidehighered.com/news/2014/04/02/students-disabilities-frustrated-ignorance-and-lack-services

—*Brittany Dreon is an advertising and public relations major.*

Racial inclusion

What to do when conflict breaks out in the classroom

"Just because I am Black I cannot speak for all my 'people.'"

"Love how my professor asks the class about the political issues w/the Oscars & I bring up Asians & she shuts me down … OK don't ask then."

"Our professor just asked the only Black girl in class if she understood what 'African time' meant."

"When your professor is so biased towards Latinas and undermines the hardships that Asians have to go through in this society."

"When your White professor tells you, 'well since you aren't African American, I wouldn't expect you to understand.' But you are African."

Racial tensions can rise abruptly in a classroom. Sometimes, the tension is due to something an instructor says: the wrong word, an awkward attempt at humor, or a stereotype laid bare. And sometimes, students argue about racial issues. Whatever the case, professors are responsible for handling these conflicts. They cannot just be ignored.

Racial tensions and protests have emerged at dozens of campuses over the mistreatment of different racial groups. Educator Caprice D. Hollins wrote a chapter called "Breaking the Cycle of Color Blindness in Higher Education" that was featured in the book "Talking About Race: Alleviating the Fear." In it, she explains that many college professors, "don't grow up having conversations about race and are not taught ways in which race matters in their own educational experience. Having little experience, education or training in race relations, combined with their fears, leaves many ill prepared to infuse race content into their curriculum." Some students believe that superficial cordiality will not solve problems, and want to see open and honest dialogue. Other students fear frank discussions about race. Such conversations can be raw and affect everyone in the room.

In many cases, race, racial groups and race relations are misunderstood and there might even be disagreement about whether a discussion is relevant to course content. But when tensions flare, the instructor must take action. Racial tensions can't be put on the back burner or rescheduled.

In one classroom, a Black student questioned a White student while she was giving a report critical of affirmative action. The professor stopped the question, saying it was the White student's time to speak. She had the two stay after class to talk. As the Black student described her view, the White student began crying. The professor blamed the Black student: "See, you made her cry." The situation deteriorated and campus police were called.

Howard C. Stevenson has also seen other situations that could have been resolved go wrong.

Stevenson is a professor of urban education and Africana studies at the University of Pennsylvania. He is former chair of the Applied Psychology and Human Development Division in the university's School of Graduate Studies.

In a seminar at Michigan State University, Stevenson said, "People can live very different realities throughout their lives … Everyone comes with a different dossier of racial experience and degree of practice." With that in mind, it is no surprise that racial tensions may arise in a classroom. They are a consequence of people not fully understanding each other. And when tensions do arise, everyone in the room, including the instructor, feels it personally or vicariously. Conflicts are not just among people, but internal as well.

Stevenson said, "the instructor might feel like avoiding the situation by denying its existence or ending it quickly. It can be a time for teaching."

Although it is human for professors to feel overwhelmed by a face-to-face racial encounter, they cannot avoid the situation or deny its effects. It is a human reaction to want to take flight or to bury feelings in such situations. According to Stevenson though, those responses are unprofessional and even unethical.

What is a professor to do when racial tensions rise?

Strategies

The best time to prepare for a surprise confrontation is before it happens. Professors can identify gaps in their race relations knowledge, decide which ones are most important on their campus and start addressing them. To narrow the gaps, professors can:

- Make friendships. Stevenson said, "Asking for help and practicing how to manage racial stress takes courage." Practice? Yes. Stevenson said, "It's like learning algebra. You don't just show up in algebra class and state your opinion, and you can't do it with race."
- Professors can seek out, meet with or work on projects with colleagues who can expand their perspectives.
- Attend relevant campus workshops, lectures and meetings of student groups.
- Read about people's perspectives.

These actions are likely to raise instructors' fluency with racial issues and increase their ability to teach, advise and discuss.

At the moment of confrontation, Stevenson advises, professors should not seek a speedy exit, but stop everything and buy 20-60 seconds to recalibrate and set up a conversation. They can say "Excuse me," "Let's talk about that," or "Let's stop here a while." Stevenson recommends rehearsing these phrases.

In the short time that follows, instructors should take a quick inventory of their own feelings. "Try not to be afraid … the stress is totally human and can be counter-productive. Pretending it doesn't affect you is human, but not helpful … Calculate your level of discomfort, locate where you feel it and tell yourself." And breathe. In "Promoting Racial Literacy in Schools: Differences That Make a Difference," Stevenson writes that relaxation builds the courage to cope.

This is the first step in RECAST: Racial Encounter Coping Appraisal and Socialization Theory.

The next step is to acknowledge the same stresses in others: "Let's talk."

The conversation has to be about issues and feelings. It is not for assigning blame. Ground rules can establish that. Stevenson advises professors to neither overreact nor underreact, and to bring calm to the chaos. This helps people listen.

Helen Fox teaches about racism, poverty, "third world" development and intercultural leadership at the University of Michigan. In her book, "When Race Breaks Out," she suggests that students agree to ground rules for conversations about race.

Her book offers 10 rules developed by some of her advanced students. Rules include:

- Assume that everyone wants to learn and understand each others' experiences.
- Listen to others. Don't talk all the time. Don't always be preparing your rebuttal or next remark. Let a few seconds elapse between exchanges; cultivate patience.
- Don't "sterilize" the discussion by playing it safe or making certain topics off-limits.
- Attack ideas, not people.

Resources

Fox, Helen. "When Race Breaks Out: Conversations about Race and Racism in College Classrooms." New York: Peter Lang, 2001.

Grineski, Steve. "Talking about Race: Alleviating the Fear." 1st ed. Sterling: Stylus Publishing, 2013.

Stevenson, Howard C. "Promoting Racial Literacy in Schools: Differences That Make a Difference." New York: Teachers College Press, 2014.

—Joe Grimm is visiting editor in residence in the School of Journalism.

#BlackOnCampus is about what goes on inside classrooms, too

"Being told by your English teacher that you're smart for a Black girl."

"When profs do not learn a Black student's name because it's 'too hard' but they can learn scientific names for plants+animals."

"Profs speak more slowly & deliberately when answering me as if I'm somehow much less intelligent than my counterparts."

"Conversing with students and profs that have spent zero amount of time considering or learning from/about our tradition."

Campus protests that began in the 2015-2016 academic year demonstrated widespread discontent among Black and African American students on campus. Thousands, both students and profs, demonstrated and wrote about their feelings on the #BlackOnCampus hashtag. That's where the comments above came from.

The movement began in September at the University of Missouri-Columbia over protests by the student government president that the university was not responsive to bigotry. The protest went national and, within three months, students at about 80 universities had issued demands about systemic and structural racism on campus.

Attention focused on university structure, policies and hiring practices. Professors do not set university policy, and some professors were part of the #BlackOnCampus movement. These are some of the demands posted on TheDemands.org that reflect how some students say professors are not connecting with them.

Claremont McKenna College: "Mandatory and periodic racial sensitivity trainings for all professors. The majority of the 20 students at the first social recalled instances in which professors made racially insensitive remarks, asked students to represent their race in class, or repeatedly mistook students for other students of color in the class."

Dartmouth: "All professors will be required to be trained in not only cultural competency but also the importance of social justice in their day-to-day work."

Duke University: "All professors, Student Affairs faculty, and DUPD must participate in cultural competency and implicit bias training overseen by the Task Force on Bias and Hate Issues."

Emory University: "We would like to see repercussions or sanctions for racist actions performed by professors, administrators/staff and students alike. Bias incident reports are not sufficient. Our micro- and macroaggressions should not be regarded as just data collection but should, in fact, be taken seriously and met with the highest level of urgency and care."

Harvard Law School: "Mandate external-organization-run diversity training programs for all professors that include (1) cultural competency and (2) models of effective contextualization—i.e., facilitated conversations about how to honor and navigate the difficulty and importance of bringing topics of race, class, nationality, gender, religion, and sexual orientation into the classroom."

Notre Dame of Maryland: "That professors incorporate volunteering into course requirements in order to be in keeping with the school's mission of social justice. And, also, to establish better connections with those in need in Baltimore."

Southern Methodist University: "Sensitivity training for all faculty and staff, including tenured professors, must be mandatory."

Strategies

Instructors do not need to wait for someone else to create a sensitivity program to begin addressing issues that can help them teach better. Besides, such programs are tough to sustain and might not be as comprehensive as the professor wants. A professor can start connecting appropriately with students on any day.

Books, film and other materials help with background knowledge, of course, but there is a greater resource: students, colleagues and friends.

Students have said they do not wish to be asked to fill in knowledge gaps for professors in terms of basic concepts and vocabulary. That's what books are for. But students are experts on their own situations. It takes relationship building to convey sincerity of interest and a safe way to exchange ideas, and student experts live on every campus.

A few topics to explore:

Definitions:Some terms, such as "White privilege," "racism," "reverse racism," "racial preferences," "cultural appropriation" and "the race card" have vastly different meanings to different people. Nothing good happens when people discuss concepts before they agree on what the words mean. Even a person's choice to identify as "Black" or "African American" or "African" can have deep meaning. These are some of the basics in "100 Questions and Answers About African Americans" in the resources at the end of this chapter.

Connections: Some Black and African American students feel much greater connection to their race than other students do to theirs. The close association can be one that was historically imposed. It can be a system that judges individuals of some groups, but not others, by other members of the group. It can be stereotyping that groups some people by race, but sees others in more dimensions.

Visibility: One element of White privilege is being able to go about the day without worrying about race-based perceptions. Black and African American students can feel acutely aware of their visibility in a class, lecture hall, on campus or in town. This can be reinforced by being singled out in class, or being called by the name of a different student who is of the same race.

Invisibility: When courses or teaching material do not include anything about a group of people, this is called symbolic annihilation. It tells people that their group doesn't exist or matter. Some of the 2015-2016 college demands were for greater cultural awareness. Professors can analyze their course material to see who created it, who is represented in it and who they are inviting in as guest speakers.

Microaggressions: These everyday slights and snubs, often unintentional, can seem so trivial that some people question whether they are real or even ridicule them as inconsequential. They include assumptions about people's experiences, interests and abilities. Ask students what microaggressions are, how often they occur and about their cumulative effects. Individual answers will likely mean more than reading the approximately 5,000 studies that have been done on microaggressions.

Resources

Brown-Glaude, Winnifred R. "Doing Diversity in Higher Education: Faculty Leaders Share Challenges and Strategies." New Brunswick: Rutgers University Press, 2008.

Michigan State University School of Journalism. "100 Questions and Answers About African Americans." Ann Arbor: Read the Spirit, 2016.

Michigan State University Office of Faculty and Organizational Development. "Inclusive Teaching Methods," directory. June 13, 2016 http://fod.msu.edu/oir/inclusive-teaching-methods

—Joe Grimm is visiting editor in residence in the School of Journalism.

Teaching the growing population of Latino students

"All migrant workers are not a 'plague' on America."
"Thanks for talking to the students making racist jokes, it made me feel comfortable knowing you were on my side."

The number of Latino and Hispanic students enrolled in two- or four-year universities has more than tripled since 1998. However, according to the Pew Research Center, "Hispanics still lag other groups in obtaining a four-year degree."

The rapid rise in Latino college enrollment has changed many campuses. Latino students are "less likely than other students to assume loans, more likely to attend part-time, and more likely to work part- or full-time to help pay for college," according to the National Conference of State Legislatures. Because Latino students are also less likely to follow a one-school, four-year plan, it should not be assumed that their experiences are just like those of students on the traditional plan.

Beside having a higher likelihood of being first-generation or transfer students, or being bilingual or from lower-income families, ethnicity and cultural identity can make Latino and Hispanic students the subject of questions.

According to researchers Flavio Francisco Marsiglia and Paz M-B Zorita, "Latino students complain (about) how they have to 'explain themselves' to their non-Latino classmates and instructors. They often use phrases such as: 'not belonging,' 'being alone,' and 'feeling as a guest' to describe their lack of connection with higher education institutions."

Latino students may feel that their heritage is underrepresented, misunderstood or disrespected by professors and students. One student shared: "A professor once went on a long rant about how migrant workers are a 'plague' on the country and should not be naturalized. My grandma was a migrant worker and I don't think my

family is destroying the country." This is a classic example
of how students might understandably take a stereotype or
generalization as a judgment about themselves or families.
Instructors cannot rely on generalities about nationality,
language, income or family history, given the diversity among
the nation's nearly 60 million Latino and Hispanic people.

The more professors know about Hispanic and Latino
students, the better they can teach all their students.

Strategies

Latino culture is one of many that highly value family
connections. Parents and students alike may have trouble
with students' new degree of geographic and emotional
freedom, especially if the student is the first family member to
go to college. Student confidentiality rules discourage direct
communication between professors and parents, but complete
and repeated communication with students can help them
explain to their families what is going on and how they are
doing. Students who do not come from a family of college
graduates might need more help learning about the resources
available on campus. The professor can have an important
role referring students to the help students say they need. Of
course, it would be premature to assume what the needs are
before knowing the students or evaluating their performance.
A clear syllabus, attachments and supplemental material about
student services can help students be successful or share
information with inquisitive parents

Integrating students' personal experience into lectures can
help reduce cultural barriers. Having students describe their
personal experiences, rather than react to others' anecdotes,
can increase participation and help foster connections
between material and student lives. Thus, lessons can have
more meaning for all students. A study at Arizona State
University found that students enrolled in a class built on
narratives connecting to the student's experiences increased
college persistence by 40 percent, helped students feel more
empowered. One student wrote, "as Hispanic students, we

often underestimate ourselves and feel intimidated by others. We must be realistic and accept that we will overcome the language barrier someday."

Stephanie Alvarez was named a U.S. Professor of the Year in 2015 by the Council for the Advancement and Support of Education. She is an associate professor of Mexican-American studies at the University of Texas—Rio Grand Valley. For her speech accepting the award she wrote, "My entire career as an educator is dedicated to flipping that paradigm of viewing Latin@ students in deficit terms upside down and to offer  students the opportunity to see themselves, their families and communities as having a wealth of assets to tap into. Students are offered the opportunity to study their culture, history, literature and produce knowledge, often alongside their own parents or with community partners. Sometimes, it is just giving the students culturally affirming material. … Every class I teach students are asked to explore and integrate their lived experiences into their research. They are engaged scholars, but they integrate engaged scholarship with the ideals of decolonial theory and Chican@ epistemology that predate the call for such engaged scholarship."

Matching students with mentors also helps students adjust. It can break down the isolation that can come from being first generation or having a non-traditional college path. A 2009 study found that "having an adviser/mentor that can help Latino students navigate the college environment will make a difference within constructs that were found to influence the intent to persist (at the college)."

According to a 2007 College Board report, Latino faculty members generally help Latino students by serving as cultural brokers. They ease the students' adjustment to the college environment; provide academic advice; serve as role models, and and prepare students to live in a global and pluralistic society. Colleges and universities can develop culturally proficient faculty members in areas of educational change. They can also offer training in critical pedagogy and encouraging exposure to diverse communities. Professors can address those needs on their own, too.

Chapters in this book about students who work, transfer or who are older might have strategies for specific situations.

Resources

Freeman, Melissa L., and Magdalena Martínez. "College Completion for Latino/a Students: Institutional and System Approaches." San Francisco: Jossey-Bass, 2015.

Kirklighter, Cristina, Diana Cárdenas, and Susan Wolff Murphy, eds. "Teaching Writing with Latino/a Students: Lessons Learned at Hispanic-Serving Institutions." Albany: State University of New York, 2007.

Michigan State University School of Journalism. "100 Questions and Answers About Hispanic and Latinos." Ann Arbor: Read the Spirit, 2014.

—Andrew DiFilippo is a packaging major.

Beyond face value: The diversity and depth of Asian Americans

"I am a proud Asian-American student. In your class, I felt like my heritage was accepted and celebrated, not tokenized or erased, but a part of a wider and vibrant community."

"Don't ask, 'What are you?' We're human beings ..."

Meaghan Kozar is a coordinator in the Office of Cultural and Academic Transitions at Michigan State University. She told of a professor who called out and separated a group of students when he was giving a test. The professor assumed they were all Chinese students intent on cheating together. The students were not Chinese, but Asian American. The issue was reported, but ultimately there were no repercussions.

Assumptions can be dangerous, and even less egregious ones can stereotype students.

One student reported instances in which professors assumed he was from China. Actually, he is Chinese-Canadian-American. Once a professor asked the student where he was from. The student began to identify Canton, a small town in metro Detroit. The professor cut him off to ask, "Canton, China?" Another time, the student was giving a group presentation. He was dressed more formally than others in his group and the professor said he could see that the student came from a more civilized country. These instances made the student feel like an outsider. "(I feel) really kind of excluded, because I feel that they don't see me as American, just as a foreigner" he said. "I don't know how to react to it. I try to shrug it off, but I am involved. I try to joke it off but at the same time it's too awkward to joke about."

Professors can help students best when they see things from a student's point of view and listen to their learners' experiences.

The Chinese-Canadian-American student once had a professor who had immigrated from Taiwan and who noticed the student's stutter. The professor told the student that his daughter also stuttered and that the student shouldn't worry about it. The student said his teacher's comment made him feel like he wasn't alone and glad that he knew this professor.

One Filipino-American said a professor who had done research in the Philippines helped her feel they had a connection. "I felt more connected to her and her teaching, because she had been able to do research in a region I was familiar with and was able to bring examples into class from her research that made me feel more connected to the material, such as jeepneys in the streets." Premature familiarity may have the opposite effect, so building rapport is advised.

Strategies

The Chinese-Canadian-American student said it is imperative that professors not judge by appearance. Many professors and other students will assume nationality from looks. "I think it's more or less ignorance," he said. "This automatic assumption is that if you look Chinese or Asian, professors assume you're an international student."

Kozar said professors struggle with relating to students and that they always need to be expanding their horizons. "I think professors in general just need to remember they were once a student," she said. "They need to constantly be challenging themselves and open to learning." She also said that to understand culture and see beyond prejudice, one needs to talk to people who are different and learn from them on a more personal level. "So how you can overcome it is by immersing yourself in their culture, not as a researcher, but as someone wanting to expand your horizons," she said. "That's how you learn, making friends who are different from you."

Phil Yu created the blog Angry Asian Man and received the 2016 Justice in Action Award from the Asian American Legal Defense and Education Fund. On a visit to Michigan State, he emphasized that professors shouldn't go by a student's looks and that Asian American culture is diverse.

He said, "There's not one Asian-American perspective because the community is very diverse and represents a lot of different histories and cultures and stories. So you can't count on anyone representing one type of Asianness, I think." He was the keynote speaker at an Activism, Politics and Social Media Summit, Raising Asian American Voices. "I think to generalize an Asian American student would be sort of a disservice."

Some have also noted that when Asian Americans on campus are discussed, those with South Asian ancestries in India, Bangladesh, Pakistan and Sri Lanka are sometimes overlooked, as are people descended from Central Asian countries.

A class at the University of Massachusetts-Boston polled Asian-American students there and found four areas of concern: student relations with professors, relations among students, difficulty being included in class discussions and, for some, language barriers.

The class made four recommendations that could help any student, not just Asian-American students.

- Make lectures available in writing and recordings online, as well as a glossary of technical terms.
- For classes heavy on participation and discussions, start with a day of icebreakers and introductions.
- Have an inclusive participation protocol that includes raising hands to be called upon or giving all students turns randomly.
- Train faculty about Asian-American communication styles and experiences of discrimination.

Effective professors are respectful and open when dealing with cultures they are unfamiliar with. They understand that each student is unique.

Resources

Gonzalez, Jennifer. "Asian-American and Pacific Islander Students Are Not Monolithically Successful, Report Says." The Chronicle of Higher Education, 2011. June 13, 2016 http://chronicle.com/article/Asian-AmericanPacific/128061/

Suyemoto, Karen. "The Asian American Classroom." University of Massachusetts-Boston, 2011. June 13, 2016 https://www.umb.edu/editor_uploads/images/asamst/Final_Report_AsAm_Classroom_Experiences.pdf

—Bryce Airgood is a journalism major.

Native Americans: Dealing with cultural misunderstandings

"Be non-biased toward ethnicities. The reason why I say that is because many people can just be culturally insensitive to not only Native Americans, but other ethnicities. But in regard to Native American specifics, never do the 'o' thing and clap your hand to your mouth. Never show up in headdresses. When talking about stereotypes, address the Native American side."

It is important that professors keep an open mind and not assume they know things about a culture when they may not. As one Aleut Native American student put it, "Just be aware that you're unaware and there's no shame in that." People outside the culture don't always understand the significance of certain events or misjudge their importance. Some professors assume they know more about Native Americans than they actually do.

It can be confusing to even know how to refer to Native people. One non-Native student tweeted, "My Early English professor just said that 'Native American' is not a politically correct term, but 'American Indian' is ... um, no." Another wrote, "There's a horrible, hair-raising kind of irony to my professor saying 'Indian' in place of 'Native American' on Columbus Day." Although the students meant well, there is no consensus among Native people about a preferred term. Many prefer "American Indian." Tribal affiliations such as Navajo or Seneca can be better, when relevant.

Another Native student has had people question his heritage. He looks Caucasian and is less than half Native. His blood quantum is still high enough for him to qualify as an enrolled tribal member. Once, when trying to explain to a professor what it was like to have such a small number of his people left, the professor expressed her belief that he was not Native. She said that he no longer had any Native genes left. The student said that the professor afterward said she was just teasing, but he did not appreciate it and expected more sensitivity from someone with a doctorate. For many nations, a 25 percent blood quantum is sufficient to be a registered member. But cultural affiliation cannot be measured in percentages. The student said it is frustrating to have professors correct him on how he self-identifies. Sometimes, when he says he is Native American, instructors will say, "Oh, you're Indian." He does not appreciate them telling him what he is, especially after he had just told them himself.

One student, a member of the Little Traverse Bay Bands of Odawa Indians, wrote that he has trouble with invasive questions such as, "How much (Native) are you?" and "Is it true that you get free school?" What is most upsetting is when people challenge his Native identity because of the way he looks. "Many times, people say to me, 'but you don't look Native American' which I find the most offensive, and I end up having to show them my tribal ID to prove that I am."

Strategies

Why are there cultural misunderstandings about Native people? It might be due to incomplete education. It could be lack of daily exposure. As one student put it, "We might as well live in the Amazon 'cause people don't think they'll meet us in real life unless they go to a reservation.

Avoiding cultural misunderstandings can be difficult. Things that offend one culture might not even be understood by another.

The Michigan State University Office of Cultural and Academic Transitions helps connect diverse peoples, programs and ideas. Its American Indian student coordinator, Patricia Dyer-Deckrow, has this advice for teaching Native American students:

- One should not assume Native students are from reservations, but if they are among the first in their families to go to college, they might need the same help as other first-generation college students. They might have to learn on their own how to use office hours, academic advising, financial aid and tutoring services.

- Students from reservations coming to large universities might have culture shock, like students coming from small towns. They might be quiet and will need to be drawn out.

- When drawing students out, don't put Native students on the spot in front of the class. Save personal questions for outside of class or during office hours.

- Don't expect Native students to know everything about Native Americans. There are more than 500 federally recognized, sovereign tribes. They vary by region and have different customs, languages and histories.

Heritage and identity are unique to each person. One person might identify as Native American while another might identify as Indian.

In Canada, indigenous people are referred to as First Nations or Aboriginal. Indian is a less accepted term there. There are many different aspects and details to know about each culture.

There is a lot of confusion on what the "correct" term is, but in the end it is a case-by-case basis and depends on what a person wants to be called. The Native Times reported that a Lakota man from the Standing Rock Sioux Reservation said, "If some Indians want to be called Native Americans or

Natives, let them be called that, but I was born an Indian and I shall die an Indian." Others feel that way, too, but not all do.

The best strategy for working with Native students is to get to know more about them so as to be better prepared in the classroom. This can happen by spending time with student organizations, in conversation with individuals and by reading about the cultures. Consider contacting campus chapters of groups such as the North American Indigenous Student Organization or the American Indians Science & Engineering Society.

However, as stated by the Native American Cultural Awareness document, "You must leave your stereotypes, prejudices, biases, and ethnocentric ideas at the door."

Resources

Eastman, Charles. "The Soul of the Indian (Native American)."Dover Publications, Inc. 2003.

Michigan State University School of Journalism and Native American Journalists Association. "100 Questions, 500 Nations: A Guide to Native America." Canton: Read the Spirit, 2014.

Native Sun News Editorial Board. "Native American vs. American Indian: Political Correctness dishonors traditional chiefs of old." Native Times, April 12, 2015. June 13, 2016 http://www.nativetimes.com/index.php/life/commentary/11389-native-american-vs-american-indian-political-correctness-dishonors-traditional-chiefs-of-old

Nerburn, Kent. "Wisdom of the Native Americans." Novato: New World Library, 1999.

—*Bryce Airgood is a journalism major.*

Ahead of the curve: Teaching toward a non-majority world

"When you taught about the Vietnam War in class, you failed to discuss about how the Hmong people were recruited by the

CIA to help Americans fight against the communists and how we were threatened for a genocide when the United States fled the war. We are a part of American history, too."

"Thank you for providing me education and teaching me to be original. Thank you for being passionate in what you do and inspiring me. Continue in doing so and don't let me down. Always guide me to understand better. Not everyone wants to be a professor, but without you, who would research and bring solutions in this world?"

Mirroring the country's population changes, college demographic in the United States, like the country's, are changing rapidly. In 2015, the US. Census Bureau reported that the nation's first age group to have no racial majority was starting school and heading for college.

The difference is not just a change in quantity. Now, the spectrum of subgroups is wider. In those states and colleges that no longer have a majority race or ethnicity, the term "minorities" is dated. Groups of people rarely represented in colleges before are registering in large numbers. For example, Hmong, Syrian, Chaldean, Somali, Bangladeshi, Muslim and Hindu students are adding variety to the growing diversity of the college population pie chart. Inclusiveness is no simple, one-dimensional question of race or nationality or religion. It is multidimensional. Note that the Pew Research Center reported in 2015 that the nation's proportion of mixed-race people was at 6.9 percent and rising.

Hmong people illustrate how some other underrepresented groups feel. Many Hmong settled in the United States after being evacuated following U.S. withdrawal from Vietnam. Parents were able to send their children to school, giving them the opportunity for a better education. Being children of immigrants, students struggled adjusting to a school system where they sometimes went unnoticed.

According to Michigan State University Hmong American Student Association President Sarah Vang, "Hmong students tend to get overlooked."

Hmong students are often frustrated by the lack of recognition about their cultures and history. "When talked about in history classes, professors hardly ever mention Hmong involvement, especially in the Vietnam war," said Vang. "This just proves how much racial injustice there is toward our community."

As an Asian ethnicity, Hmong students are often treated as a subcategory and then judged against the larger group. "Microaggressions are hurtful for anyone," said Vang. "They are especially hurtful when professors say things to us like, 'your eyes are too big for an Asian.'"

Arab students and Muslims are often conflated, with Christian Arabs assumed to be Muslim and Muslim Indians assumed to be Arabs.

There are interest groups for Somali students at the University of Minnesota, Bangladeshi students at Wayne State University in Detroit and Chaldean students at the University of Michigan. One day, members of these groups will be more familiar as they have larger roles in the general population. But understanding and change is required now, when these students are in class.

Instructors, like others in the general population, have little knowledge or training about the myriad cultures and religions now represented in universities, but have to get it soon.

Strategies

The first step in conducting a multicultural classroom is to abandon assumptions. Although it is natural to see people from our own frames of reference and convenient to categorize them, it is better to do what great professors have always done: treat students as individuals.

The next step, after holding assumptions in check, is to learn about new groups. Individuals can share identities, histories and values with others. To learn how their campus is changing, faculty can take advantage of student organizations. Attending a group's public cultural event or regular meeting can help with understanding. In some cases, another faculty member of a specialized ethnic studies program on campus can be a bridge.

There are also ways to plan teaching so that students from any race, culture or religion can respond to it.

Harvard's Derek Bok Center for Teaching and Learning offers many tips on teaching diverse classes. Beyond replacing assumptions with information, the center suggests dozens of tips under several categories:

- Develop a syllabus that explores multiple perspectives on topics.
- Design instruction and materials with diversity in mind.
- Get to know students as individuals.
- Design respectful and meaningful student interactions.
- Encourage participation.

The Bok Center sheet also offers further advice on how to intervene in racially charged situations.

The Michigan State University Office of Faculty and Organizational Development offers a list of readings about inclusive teaching methods. It is at http://fod.msu.edu/oir/inclusive-teaching-methods

The benefit of inclusive teaching methods is that they do not have to be revamped every time someone from a new culture arrives in the classroom. The goal is to achieve an inclusive atmosphere so that everyone can learn the content and about each other.

Resources

Dallalfar, Arlene, Esther Kingston-Mann, and R. Timothy Sieber. "Transforming Classroom Culture: Inclusive Pedagogical Practices." New York: Palgrave Macmillan, 2011.

Harvard University Derek Bok Center for Teaching and Learning. "Teaching in Racially Diverse College Classrooms." 2010. June 13, 2016 http://isites.harvard.edu/fs/html/icb.topic58474/TFTrace.html

—Meaghan Markey is an advertising management and public relations major.

Assumptions about identity are no substitute for knowing

"When you returned my article with a note that said 'Writing in a second language is tough, but you're getting there,' I believed it for a second. For a second I forgot about the first-place award I'd won for writing the week before. After reading your comments about my ineptitude in my native language, I questioned my proficiency and forgot about the three other languages in which I can also adeptly write and speak. Somehow, your crooked compliment made me fail to recall the praise, A's, 'oohs' and 'aahs' that my work had garnered for so many years. I thought I wasn't 'there.' But I quickly realized that you were wrong. You crafted the worst, most inaccurate criticism I've ever received and drew your conclusion from the tone of my skin and curly hair instead of from errors in my conjugation and syntax. That disrespected me on so many levels. I am an American. I was born in the United States. Don't look at me and make assumptions about who I am or where I'm from. And don't use your classroom to turn prejudicial tendencies into self-fulfilling prophecies."

This case represents overlapping problems. One problem is an appearance-based assumption about citizenship and origins. The first assumption was compounded by the second, that people who look like this student must come from countries where English is not well known.

These assumptions point to the issue of labeling. Even if the English-language learner label had been correct, labels lump students into categories that preclude individual teaching interventions.

In addition, the teacher did not provide complete feedback. The critique should have cited examples in the student's work but instead was based on inaccurate assumptions. It was taken as a personal, inaccurate attack. The student dropped the class.

Strategies

"Seven Principles for Good Practice in Undergraduate Education" has been widely circulated since being published in the March 1987 bulletin of the American Association for Higher Education. It is on many university websites.

The principles are:

- Encourage contact between students and faculty.
- Develop reciprocity and cooperation among students.
- Encourage active learning.
- Give prompt feedback.
- Emphasize time on task.
- Communicate high expectations.
- Respect diverse talents and ways of learning.

Arthur W. Chickering and Zelda F. Gamson wrote and explained the principles listed. Chickering was director of the Center for the Study of Higher Education at Memphis State University. Gamson was a sociologist with the University of Massachusetts' John W. McCormack Institute of Public Affairs and the Center for the Study of Higher and Postsecondary Education at the University of Michigan.

The incident that this student wrote about violated several of these principles.

Applying some of the principles could have prevented the problem. For example, the teacher could have used Chickering and Gamson's principle for greater contact with students.

Assumptions are no substitute for knowledge and assessment. If the teacher had found out about the student's writing, she would not have made the assumptions she did. The case shows vividly that instructors are out of bounds when they assume a student's national origin or experience and make judgments about performance based on those guesses.

Professors can understand "diverse talents and ways of learning" only if they know their students. Chickering and Gamson wrote that, "while each practice can stand alone on its own, when all are present their effects multiply." Conversely, the absence of several teaching principles can multiply misunderstandings, too.

At the end of the letter, the student wrote that prejudices had created self-fulfilling prophecies in the professor's mind. This is a twist on the often-cited Pygmalion or Rosenthal Effect, that instructors' positive expectations can help students perform better, while negative expectations can hold them back. Ironically, Pygmalion is the name of a George Bernard Shaw play in which a professor of phonetics makes a bet that he can teach a London flower girl to speak proper English.

Resources

Chickering, Arthur W., and Zelda F. Gamson. "Seven Principles for good practice in undergraduate education." AAHE Bulletin, 39, 3-7, 1987. June 13, 2016 http://www.lonestar.edu/multimedia/SevenPrinciples.pdf

Cooper, H. M. "Pygmalion Grows Up: A Model for Teacher Expectation Communication and Performance Influence." Review of Educational Research, 49, 389-410, 1979. June 13, 2016 http://rer.sagepub.com/content/49/3/389

—*Joe Grimm is visiting editor in residence in the School of Journalism.*

Religious inclusion

Religious holiday requests require flexibility, discernment

"I felt like I had to choose between my grades and my religion, but what's worse, I don't know which my parents will be more upset about."

"It was the first time that I had been given an ultimatum. It was either attend my holiday and accept I would no longer be able to receive the grade I expected in the course or accept missing my religious holiday and still have the chance at a satisfying grade in the class."

"'You're done starving yourself so now you want to miss class?' The professor's words lingered in the air as I sat in complete shock and embarrassment."

The student who made the first comment often wore a Star of David necklace and clothing from a Jewish summer camp. She always sat at the front of her 30-person class. She asked the teacher to reschedule an exam so she could observe Yom Kippur, part of the Jewish High Holidays. The professor emailed her a makeup date. She replied that the new date would conflict with her class schedule. The professor responded: "To avoid this in the future, I recommend you prioritize your class exams and your religious activities. It seems to have caused you conflict." The professor gave her another option, but his remark about priorities stung. The student felt he had shown disrespect for her beliefs.

The student who made the second comment was affiliated with the Little River Band of Ottawa Indians and said she asked a professor to reschedule an exam so she could attend a Ghost Supper. In her tribe, the community gathers in someone's home to honor ancestors. She said she explained that it was a religious and cultural experience. The professor was adamant about her not missing the exam. The student did not want to be penalized, so she panicked and skipped the event. Later, an adviser told the student that the Ghost Supper should have been excusable as a religious holiday. By then, the student was reluctant to ask other professors to be excused for religious events because she did not want to go through the process of explaining and still being refused.

The student who wrote the third note had asked to be excused for Eid al-Fitr, the end of the holy month of Ramadan during which observant Muslims pray and fast. The professor responded, "You're done starving yourself and now you want to miss class?" The professor thought of his response as just a playful joke, but the student felt mocked and belittled.

A scolding, a denial and a joke about religion. There must be better answers.

College campuses, scheduled around major Christian holidays, today are admitting students with other religions and practices. Non-Christian holidays may be unfamiliar, may require different accommodations, and may not be anchored to the secular calendar. They may complicate professors' decisions. As their employers, university administrators have the same issues with faculty and staff. Policies can guide, but cannot anticipate every situation and need.

Strategies

With growing religious diversity and an increased desire to respect varying needs, universities offer discretion rather than directions. At Michigan State University, the policy is "the faculty and staff should be sensitive to the observance of these holidays so that students who absent themselves from classes on these days are not seriously disadvantaged. ... In the absence of a simple and dignified way to determine the validity of individual claims, the claim of a religious conflict should be accepted at face value."

Similarly, Arizona State University directs that, "the community should in all its activities be sensitive to the religious practices of the various religious faiths represented in its student body and employees." That policy suggests rescheduling, voluntary substitutions, job reassignments and modification of grooming requirements. Not all religious accommodations have to do with schedules.

Some instructors build flexibility for religious holidays and other needs into the syllabus. Most schedules allow religious holidays to be taken as excused absences and some professors allow a couple of penalty-free unexcused absences. In some syllabi, students—all of them—may be allowed to drop their one or two lowest grades.

Attendance and due-date policies that are flexible, equitable for all students and published in the syllabus can prevent misunderstandings. The University of Denver advises: "Faculty are asked to be responsive to requests when students contact them IN ADVANCE to request such an excused absence. Students are responsible for completing assignments given during their absence, but should be given an opportunity to make up work missed because of religious observance."

Accommodation implies that students who miss a class or postpone an exam for a religious holiday should not be penalized for observing their holidays. In some faiths, important holidays can make students miss several classes in a row. To support religious diversity, rather than just tolerate it, it must be possible for students to catch up on content they miss. That can mean getting notes, material or recordings from other students or meeting with the instructor. A teacher can anticipate that by including a section on attendance and religious observance in the syllabus.

Resources

Matlins, Stuart M., and Arthur J. Magida. "How to Be a Perfect Stranger: The Essential Religious Etiquette Handbook." Woodstock: SkyLight Paths Publishing, 2003.

Michigan State University School of Journalism. "100 Questions and Answers About American Jews with a Guide to Religious Holidays." Ann Arbor: Read the Spirit, 2016.

Michigan State University, School of Journalism "100 Questions and Answers About Muslim Americans with a Guide to Religious Holidays." Ann Arbor: Read the Spirit, 2014.

—Christina Briones is a communication major with public relations and Spanish minors. Contributor Bryce Airgood is a journalism major.

Holidays that university calendars might not include

University student bodies, staff and faculty have become more diverse. More people have religious holidays that fall outside of mandated days off or that have longer periods of observance. Flexibility and a little advance knowledge helps. To prevent surprises, this chapter highlights religious holidays that might not be reflected in university schedules.

Though world religions differ in specific rituals and holidays, almost all have times set aside for fasting, prayer and celebrations. Academic tests, group presentations and outside meetings may have greater attendance and rates of success if they are scheduled when they will not conflict with religious observances.

First, a few notes:

- Dates for most holidays vary from the Gregorian calendar.
- In the Jewish, Islamic and Bahá'í religions, days begin at sunset and end at the next sunset.
- Observance traditions can vary by country and region.
- Not all members of a religion observe its holidays in the same way.

Extended holiday periods

Many academic calendars note single-day holidays, but some religious festival periods do not permit work over several days. Students might ask to be absent during individual days or throughout these periods.

Jewish

Passover: Passover typically occurs in the spring, and the first, second, seventh and eighth days of Passover do not permit work. An extensive seder (shared feast) is often attended or hosted on the first night of Passover.

Sukkot: A festival of the harvest, work is forbidden on both the first and second days of Sukkot.

Rosh Hashanah and Yom Kippur: A period known as the High Holidays, in the fall, actually encompasses several important holidays: Rosh Hashanah (the Jewish New Year), 10 days known as the Ten Days of Repentance, and finally, Yom Kippur. Work is not permitted on Rosh Hashanah or on Yom Kippur, and Rosh Hashanah is celebrated over two days.

Bahá'í

Ridvan: During the festival of Ridvan, the first, ninth and 12th days are considered holy, and work is not permitted.

Jain

Paryushan Parva: The deepest spiritual period of the year, the Festival of Forgiveness lasts eight or 10 days, during which time Jains fast, study and meditate. Vegetarianism and nonviolence are primary Jain teachings.

Individual days when work is not permitted
Jewish

Shemini Atzeret, Simchat Torah and Shavuot: Work is not permitted on these holidays for those who observe them.

Bahá'í

Naw-Ruz, Ridvan (first, ninth and 12th days), Declaration of the Bab, Ascension of Bahá'u'lláh, Martyrdom of the Bab, Birth of the Bab and Birth of Bahá'u'lláh: In the Bahá'í faith, nine holy days do not permit work. Chronologically, these days begin in the spring with the Bahá'í New Year (Naw-Ruz) and extend to late autumn, with the Birth of Bahá'u'lláh.

Days of fasting

Day-long or days-long fasting periods are common in several world religions. Tests and other intensive projects may be best placed outside of these fasting periods.

Christian

Ash Wednesday and Good Friday: Many Western Christians limit their meals on Ash Wednesday (the start of Lent) and on Good Friday (the one before Easter Sunday).

Nativity Fast and Fast of Great Lent: Eastern Orthodox Christians undergo the 40-day Nativity Fast prior to Christmas, and the Fast of Great Lent prior to Pascha (Easter).

The Eastern Orthodox Christian Lenten fast lasts longer and is much stricter than the Western Christian Lent, forbidding several foods on most days and all food on specific days.

Muslim

Ramadan: Ramadan is the 30-day sunrise-to-sunset fast widely known outside of Islam, and all physically able and of-age Muslims are required to fast during the entirety of Ramadan—without even a drop of water between sunrise and sunset. Work and school are permitted, but people who have not eaten all day will likely want to break their fast at sunset. Being in class while people are snacking or eating can be a challenge. Being unable to eat as soon as the daily fast ends can be challenging, too. Ramadan, a time of reflection, improvement and devotion, is set according to the lunar calendar.

Jewish

Yom Kippur and Tisha B'Av: Major public fast days are Yom Kippur (the Day of Atonement) and Tisha B'Av (the saddest day on the Jewish calendar). Major fasts last 25 hours, and forbid food and drink. Jews also annually observe four less restrictive, minor fast days.

Hindu

Maha Shivaratri and Krishna Janmashtami and Ramanavami: Hindu fasting may be performed for various reasons, though notably for Maha Shivaratri, Krishna Janmashtami and Ramanavami. Generally, Hindu fasts are not as rigid as those of other religions and may sometimes just limit the types of foods that adherents can eat.

Bahá'í

Nineteen-Day Fast: Typically in March, this fast suspends food and drink from sunrise to sunset.

Common pilgrimages

Smaller pilgrimages are common in many faiths, but some annual pilgrimages are so large that they set world records in human migration. Some pilgrimages are to holy places, while others are occasions for homecoming.

Muslim

Hajj: This is the annual Islamic pilgrimage to Mecca in Saudi Arabia. One pillar of Islam states that every able Muslim must perform the Hajj at least once. Upward of 1 million adherents travel for Hajj each year, and while the pilgrimage lasts approximately five days, many pilgrims arrive early, stay late, or both.

Hindu

Kumbh Mela: The Kumbh Mela gathers millions of Hindus to bathe in a sacred river. Four sites are recognized as the Kumbh Melas, and host by rotation. At a given place, the Kumbh Mela is held every 12 years.

Buddhist

Obon: During July and August, regions of Japan and Japanese communities worldwide observe Obon, an ancient festival for one's ancestors. This is a Buddhist festival, though many non-Buddhists commemorate it, as well.

Lunar New Year

The largest annual human migration in the world, millions travel home for the Lunar New Year. Although many are familiar with this as the Chinese New Year, it is celebrated by people of many countries. The migration and festivities last several weeks.

Major days of celebration
Hindu

Diwali: The Festival of Lights arrives as winter begins, bringing family gatherings and widespread celebrations over several days.

Krishna Janmashtami: Hindus worship the deity Lord Krishna with a full day and night of events. In some regions, festivities continue longer.

Muslim

Of all Islamic holidays, only two are recognized universally: the Eids.

Eid al-Fitr: Known as the "Lesser Eid," this is the Feast of the Breaking of the Fast, celebrated immediately after Ramadan is over. More than one billion Muslims observe Eid al-Fitr, most commonly with religious services, family gatherings and fairs. Eid al-Fitr is observed for at least one day and, by many, for multiple days.

Eid al-Adha: The "Greater Eid" is the Feast of the Sacrifice, commemorated during Hajj. Many families gather on this occasion. Celebrations may last one to four days.

All-night vigils
Muslim

Laylat al-Qadr: Observed on one or more of the last 10 odd-numbered nights of Ramadan, this is regarded as the night "better than one thousand months." Many Muslims attempt to stay awake in prayer as much as possible.

Hindu

Maha Shivaratri: For this winter Hindu holiday, many devotees of Lord Shiva hold an all-night vigil.

Jewish

Shavuot: Many Jews celebrate the reception of the Torah by engaging in all-night Torah study. This is said to correct the behavior of ancient Israelites who overslept on the morning it was received.

Daily prayer times
Jewish
Orthodox Jews pray four times each day.
Muslim
Each day, facing the direction of Mecca, observant Muslims pray five times: *Fajr* (pre-dawn); *Dhuhr* (mid-day); *Asr* (afternoon); *Maghrib* (sunset) and *Isha'a* (night). Specific times vary by location and some Muslims combine prayers.
Weekly services
Jewish
The Jewish Shabbat is observed from a few minutes before sunset on Friday evening until the appearance of the first three stars in the sky on Saturday night. Shabbat begins with lighted candles and a recited blessing.
Muslim
On Fridays, Muslims offer prayer in congregation in the early afternoon (*Jumu'ah*).
Christian
On Sunday mornings, many Christians attend services with a local congregation.
Holidays, fasts and celebrations by season
(Dates vary annually.)
Fall
Paryushan Parva (Jain), Rosh Hashanah (Jewish), Yom Kippur (Jewish), Sukkot (Jewish), Birth of the Bab (Bahá'í), Shemini Atzeret (Jewish), Simchat Torah (Jewish), Birth of Bahá'u'lláh (Bahá'í), Nativity Fast (Orthodox Christian)
Winter
Diwali (Hindu/Sikh/Jain), Tu B'Shvat (Jewish), Kumbh Mela (Hindu), Lunar New Year (Chinese), Ash Wednesday (Christian), Maha Shivaratri (Hindu), Great Lent (Orthodox Christian), Nineteen-Day Fast (Bahá'í)
Spring
Naw-Ruz (Bahá'í), Passover (Jewish), Lent (Christian), Great Lent (Orthodox Christian), Ramanavami (Hindu), Ridvan (Bahá'í), Good Friday (Christian)

Summer

Declaration of the Bab (Bahá'í), Ascension of Bahá'u'lláh (Bahá'í), Shavuot (Jewish), Martyrdom of the Bab (Bahá'í), Obon (Buddhist), Tisha B'Av (Jewish), Krishna Janmashtami (Hindu)

Stephanie Fenton has provided the nation's only daily coverage of religious holidays, festivals and milestones for ReadTheSpirit online magazine and publishing company since 2007. She was an editor with the Detroit area's Suburban Lifestyles Community Newspapers and she has covered religion for AnnArbor.com.

Students singled out as Jewish, even when they're not

"My professor just told me that I look Jewish …"

"Every time my professor calls on me he always has to comment on how I have a good Jewish last name. I'm not even Jewish …"

"My professor just did a horrible racist Jewish guy impression."

"My professor just asked me if I celebrated Thanksgiving bc I'm Jewish … Dude I'm still American."

Jewish students can find their religion challenged in class, even when the class has nothing to do with religion. A teacher's response can be an assumption based on name or appearance. A remark can be an attempt to establish a connection or to be funny. It is not always appreciated and is often awkward.

And the fact is, American Jews are diverse in appearance and practice. They can be unnoticed in the classroom.

One student reported that a professor covering post-Holocaust immigration said, "It was like an invasion of the Jews—well at least the ones that were left—and you just couldn't escape it." And, according to one study, many Jewish students cannot escape discrimination on campus. The 2014 survey of 1,157 Jewish students across 55 U.S. colleges found 54 percent had experienced or witnessed anti-Semitism in the previous six months. The report was published by Trinity

College in Connecticut and the Brandeis Center. The study's definition of anti-Semitism was prejudice or discrimination involving bigotry, bullying, defamation, stereotype or hate crimes. It included both classic prejudice and political anti-Semitism related to Israel. Trinity research professor Barry Kosmin wrote that while the incidents were mostly minor, they were widespread. Researchers said the data suggest the discrimination occurred in conversation and comments rather than through vandalism or attacks. Some incidents involved taking a comment personally during a political discussion.

A University of Michigan student wrote this about a campus protest comparing Israeli politics to South African apartheid: "I walked outside of my lecture hall and onto the Diag, the heart of Michigan's campus, to see an 'Apartheid Wall' and a mock checkpoint with an intimidating student dressed as a soldier, yelling at me as I walked by. Later, I attended class on Israel's history taught by a professor who claims that Jews invented religious persecution, that the efforts and tactics of the terrorists of the Intifadas parallel those of the Maccabees, and that the recent terrorism in Israel is just a legitimate reaction to Israeli 'oppression and occupation.' By the end of the day, I felt utterly powerless, afraid, and alone."

The AMCHA group, created by two professors, has linked some activities of the "Boycott, Divestment, and Sanctions" movement, which opposes Israeli policies regarding Palestine, to anti-Semitism. Often, political discussions about actions of the Israeli government seem to cross over or open the door to anti-Semitism. While political debate about all sorts of issues is a valuable part of college life, hate speech is not. Among the Trinity/Brandeis report's recommendations was one for faculty training. Instructors need to know where the line is between legitimate debate and hate speech, to observe it and, in some cases, to redirect discussions away from hate.

Strategies

The student confronted at the mock checkpoint had a different feeling than non-Jewish students, no doubt. It felt personal. The professor's remarks magnified or intensified the student's reaction. Every classroom moment happens within the context of the larger world and every student walks into class with a different frame of reference and experience.

So, one strategy for sensitivity is to keep up with ongoing religious issues on campus and in the country. Current events and problems may frame the way messages are received.

Students say that instructors are sometimes the source of anti-Semitic comments and such cases have made headlines. Research shows, however, that most incidents are among students. Instructors, then, have responsibilities for what goes on in the classroom.

Yad Vashem, the Holocaust Martyr's and Heroes' Remembrance Authority established by the Israeli Knesset, issued a 34-page guide for teachers about addressing anti-Semitism. Suggestions include:

- Establish a constructive environment with ground rules. Agree on definitions.
- Be patient. Give the topic time, refer back when necessary and look for the best way to have the discussion with the class.
- Recognize different Jewish perspectives, but do not generalize one perspective to all Jews.
- Don't appear to condone anti-Semitism by ignoring it.
- Avoid victimization by treating people as individuals.
- Call in help if it is needed.

Resources

Michigan State University School of Journalism. "100 Questions and Answers About American Jews with a Guide to Religious Holidays." Ann Arbor: Read the Spirit, 2016.

Mulhere, Kaitlin. "Bias Reported in Survey of Jewish College Students." Inside Higher Ed, Feb. 24, 2015.

Vashem, Yad. "Addressing Anti-Semitism: Why and How? A Guide for Educators." 2007. June 13, 2016 http://www.yadvashem.org

—Christina Briones is a communication major with public relations and Spanish minors.

'I hope you're not hiding any guns under your headscarf today'

"I can't believe my professor just asked this girl from Saudi Arabia if she was a terrorist!!"

"My professor just asked if I speak Arabic and then told me I look like a terrorist ..."

"When you report a professor for saying hateful comments about Muslims and the school won't do anything about it ..."

Muslims in the United States have faced increased discrimination since the Sept. 11, 2001, terrorist attacks. American Muslims were killed along with non-Muslims in the attacks and became targets of a backlash.

International students who are Muslim can be targets of discrimination, too. Some Muslim international students come from countries where there have been terrorist attacks, often targeting other Muslims. The FBI reports that hate crimes against Muslims are up, and the Pew Research Center reports that acceptance of Muslims is down. Anti-Muslim discrimination has found a home on campuses and in classrooms, just as it has in the larger population.

Michigan Radio reporter Jennifer Guerra told the story of Imam Sohail Chaudhry, who serves at a mosque next to the Michigan State University campus. Guerra reported that shortly after the 2015 Paris bombings at the concert hall and soccer stadium, a Muslim college student went to Chaudhry for counseling. Chaudhry told Guerra that the student "said to me that her professor came into the class one day and jokingly said to her, 'I hope you're not hiding guns under your headscarf today.'" The student took her embarrassment and her hurt to the mosque across the street, not to the university.

Arabs, South Asians, Chaldeans, Sikhs and others get lumped together as Muslims, and members of all these groups have been accused, or suspected, of complicity in events to which they have no connection. News coverage and speculation connecting terror attacks globally to Islamic fundamentalism has inflamed passions. Recent rhetoric by politicians and lawmakers has emboldened people to make defamatory remarks about Muslims and act out against them. Organized Islamophobia has fanned the flames of this kind of discrimination.

On campus, anti-Muslim sentiments have been expressed in jokes about terrorism, or openly displayed in graffiti, direct discrimination, death threats and attacks. Anti-Muslim incidents on campus have been covered in national media and students have created groups to support and defend Muslim students. The Christian Science Monitor asked in January 2016 whether a campus movement in defense of Muslim students would be the next student rights movement to arise on campus.

In an environment where people are targeted just because someone thinks they are Muslim, jokes and offhand remarks perpetuate a climate that can be at least distracting for all students and even dangerous for a few. Rather than joke about it, instructors should be prepared to address anti-Muslim rhetoric and action on campus or in class.

Strategies

Islamophobic remarks can become a time for teaching. A professor's job begins by becoming informed and, when it is appropriate, informing students. Some basic knowledge:

- The first step is to challenge the connection some try to make between religion and political violence. Muslims have widely condemned terrorism done in the name of their religion. Others have not, because they are no more connected to the violence than anyone else. They feel that condemning or apologizing for something they

- Muslims are numerous, diverse and misunderstood. Muslims are often associated with Arabs, but the countries with the largest Muslim populations in the world are Indonesia, India, Pakistan, Bangladesh and Nigeria. Three of the next five countries with large Muslim populations are Arab: Egypt, Algeria and Morocco. Each has less than 5 percent of the world's 1.2 billion Muslims.
- Of the 325 million people in the United States, about 2 percent are Muslim. About half of them are U.S.-born. That proportion is growing. While many associate Muslims with Arab countries, most Arab Americans are Christian and most American Muslims are not Arabs.
- Headscarves fascinate us. A professor left Wheaton College, a Christian institution, amid the controversy that ensued when she said Christians and Muslims have the same God. Photographs of her wearing a scarf in solidarity with Muslims were widely published. The scarf, one of many styles of modest dress, is the most common on U.S. campuses. Wearing a head scarf is a matter of choice. Forty percent of American Muslim women say they do not wear hijab. Another 24 percent say they wear it sometimes.

There are several additional steps professors can take to include Muslim students. If your university has a local mosque or a Muslim studies program, consider visiting. Most mosques welcome interest by non-Muslims and can set up an orientation or introduction to Islam and to the issues Muslims face. A visit can be an opportunity to meet a resource person.

Each year, check and then note when the Islamic holy month of Ramadan occurs. Most observant Muslims will fast from sunup to sundown for the entire month. Professors show awareness if they let Muslim students break their day of fasting, even during class. Avoid embarrassment by not bringing treats for the class during Ramadan if there are Muslim students in class.

Jack Shaheen, recipient of two Fulbright teaching awards and a professor for 30 years, has written and spoken extensively about stereotyping of Muslims and Arabs. His book, "Reel Bad Arabs" and accompanying video, provide a good grounding in stereotypes as perpetuated in popular culture.

Shaheen's work suggests that instructors who make or permit jokes about Arab or Muslim terrorists can upset students and disturb their sense of safety and belonging. So can the misuse of words like jihad or fatwa, which have rich and complicated meanings.

Resources

Bishop, Tyler. "Being Muslim on Campus." The Atlantic, Nov. 20, 2015. June 13, 2016 http://www.theatlantic.com/politics/archive/2015/11/muslim-students-university/416994/

Michigan State University, School of Journalism. "100 Questions and Answers About Muslim Americans with a Guide to Religious Holidays." Ann Arbor: Read the Spirit, 2014.

Shaheen, Jack G. "Reel Bad Arabs: How Hollywood Vilifies a People." Northampton: Olive Branch, 2009.

—Eric Straughn is an international relations major and public relations minor.

Christians can find their beliefs challenged on campus

"When you told me to 'leave my faith at the door for this class and have an open mind' I have never been stunned and hurt so much in a classroom setting. My faith is more important to me than some silly assignment. Just because my beliefs are different than yours doesn't give you the right to discriminate against me, especially in your position."

"In the position you are in as a professor you have the ability to encourage people, but not if you teach in a condemning and hurtful way."

Like society, campuses are being divided over religiously politicized issues such as evolution, sexual orientation, abstinence and evangelical values. Some Christian students may feel targeted in discussions of divisive issues. New York Times' reporter Nicholas Kristof wrote that George Yancey, a sociology professor at the University of North Texas, told him, "Outside of academia I faced more problems as a Black … But inside academia I face more problems as a Christian, and it is not even close."

In an interview with Christian Post, Yancey said, "People with Christianophobia at least superficially value the ideals of religious neutrality. They perceive themselves as non-biased. So while they want to exclude Christians from the public square, they are unlikely to support measures that overtly single out Christians for punishment. This allows them to hold on to a social identity that is linked to 'tolerance'."

Yancey said these perceptions might seem to sanction decisions that seem anti-Christian. For example, in 2014, the California State University system "derecognized" 23 InterVarsity Christian Fellowship chapters on 19 campuses. The student chapters were derecognized because they required leaders to be adherents of a certain faith. This seemed to violate church and state separation at the publicly supported university. In 2011, private and non-sectarian Vanderbilt University had derecognized several student organizations that it said violated its nondiscrimination policies. Loss of recognition can mean a loss of meeting space and funding available to other student-run organizations.

The predominance of liberal viewpoints on some faculties occasionally emerges in disrespectful remarks about conservatives and evangelical Christians.

For example, one student blogged, "As I sit in this class for 50 minutes three times a week, listening to you disrespect my God and poke fun at the most important truths in my life, I can't help but get angry. I find myself with my arms crossed, my mouth terse and my head shaking. ... I can't tell you the amount of sassy letters I've written to you in my head, or the number of times I've imagined storming out of your classroom."

Another described the disrespect and condescension he felt when a professor mimicked the stereotype of a Christian pastor by waving his hands around, taking out a handkerchief, waving that around, dabbing his forehead with it, and yelling out a big "Hallelujah."

That echoed a remark that The Times' Kristof reported from another Black evangelical professor, Harvard's Jonathan L. Walton: "The same arguments I hear people make about evangelicals sound so familiar to the ways people often describe folk of color, i.e. politically unsophisticated, lacking education, angry, bitter, emotional, poor."

Speaking about a professor who seemed to convey those beliefs, one student asked, "How can I get a good grade in his class when he thinks I'm stupid because I wear a cross around my neck?"

Kristof wrote, "When perspectives are unrepresented in discussions, when some kinds of thinkers aren't at the table, classrooms become echo chambers rather than sounding boards—and we all lose."

Strategies

Setting an environment that is challenging yet supportive for all students is one key to teaching success. Religious tolerance is part of that. Yet the stereotype of the intolerant Christian occasionally seems to justify a response that is, in itself, intolerant.

As with other situations, the problem is not just comments directed at individual students, but intolerance toward the group in general, which students might take personally.

Yancey, the professor who said he faces more problems on campus for his religion than his race, said that a lesson in tolerance came during the 2016 presidential campaign when Bernie Sanders, a Jewish social democrat, was invited to speak at Liberty University, a Christian university founded by Moral Majority leader Jerry Falwell. Yancey wrote that a Liberty professor told him that the university's philosophy is to maintain a politically conservative campus, but to expose students to other ideas. That, Yancey said, should be the ideal at all universities, rather than to ridicule or sideline contrary viewpoints. It is a lot to ask students to do that, or to go one-on-one with a professor, but bringing in highly qualified guests, as Liberty did, can help create a supportive environment.

Resources

Nussbaum, Martha Craven. "The New Religious Intolerance: Overcoming the Politics of Fear in an Anxious Age." Cambridge: Belknap Press of Harvard University Press, 2012.

Smietana, Bob. "Many Evangelicals Wary of Faith Requirements for Campus Groups." Christianity Today, May 6, 2015. June 13, 2016 http://www.christianitytoday.com/gleanings/2015/may/many-evangelicals-wary-campus-groups-intervarsity-lifeway.html

—Brittany Dreon is an advertising and public relations major.

International community

Making international students feel at home away from home

"It took me a lot of hard work and talent to make it into a Big Ten school; I expect to be treated that way."

Enrollments of international students are growing in U.S. colleges and universities, contributing substantially to schools' budgets. Universities that now depend on international students would suffer financially if that trend reversed. Yet, international students often feel marginalized and belittled.

How large is the international student population? According to the Institute of International Education, "the number of international students at U.S. colleges and universities had the highest rate of growth in 35 years, increasing by 10 percent to a record high of 974,926 students in the 2014/15 academic year."

According to the institute's annual Open Doors report, China remained the top source of international students in the United States with 304,040, but that growth was outpaced by India, which grew 29.4 percent to 132,888. That was the greatest enrollment increase in India since the project began in 1954/1955.

International students and their families pay substantial sums of money to make the United States the No. 1 host of international education. However, cultural differences between International and U.S. schools in learning styles and classroom etiquette cause friction.

International enrollment at U.S. colleges and universities at record high

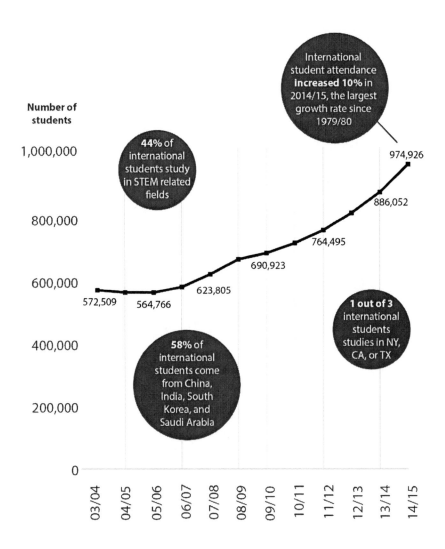

Number of students

International student attendance **increased 10%** in 2014/15, the largest growth rate since 1979/80

44% of international students study in STEM related fields

58% of international students come from China, India, South Korea, and Saudi Arabia

1 out of 3 international students studies in NY, CA, or TX

1,000,000 — 974,926

886,052

800,000

764,495

690,923

623,805

600,000

572,509   564,766

400,000

200,000

0

03/04 04/05 05/06 06/07 07/08 08/09 09/10 10/11 11/12 12/13 13/14 14/15

illustration by Matthew Hus   source: The Institute of International Education, 2015

For example, in many of the students' home countries, they are taught, as a mark of respect, not to ask too many questions and to maintain a strictly formal relationship with their professors. When American professors assume that silence means that a student doesn't know what is going on in the classroom that may lead to problems:

- Student learning is affected by how students believe they are perceived and approached by instructors. For example, when international students believe that a teacher assumes that their silence indicates a lack of understanding, the students, in turn, may assume that the instructor doubts their intelligence or abilities. Consequently, when they are ignored in the classroom, international students may feel like they are not learning anything and are being left out of the process.

- International students may be apprehensive to approach instructors about their concerns or doubts. When students get the impression that professors think of them as less competent or intelligent, they are less likely to ask for help or bring up concerns.

- There also seems to be a disconnect between U.S. students and international students. Thus, there is very little interaction between the groups. The inability to interact may interfere with group work, in-class discussions and participation.

International students may be surprised that even though they are treated as though they are behind, U.S. students and professors reveal shortcomings of their own. One student wrote this To My Professor message: "Africa is a continent, not a country, and it has hundreds of different cultures. Please don't expect me to speak for them all."

Strategies
There are many reasons instructors and students might feel disconnected. Cultural and language differences can lead to misunderstandings and uncertainty which in turn add to the

challenge of communicating with students. Here are some strategies:

- Instead of singling out international students to ask if they need extra help, make a general invitation to the class and wait to be approached. Don't make international students feel cornered or called out.
- If students seem to be struggling with an idea or process, professors can explain that it is typical for certain content to be challenging to all students.
- If there is group work, it should be explained before it is assigned because the way the group is to operate might be unfamiliar to some students. Give students opportunities to work together and mingle in class before they have to meet outside of class. Professors can check to make sure all group members are following instructions.
- Don't expect international students to represent their entire culture.
- When students approach professors, it takes questions and listening to understand their struggles. Non-academic issues can have a bearing on their work.
- Attend events hosted by your university's office for international students to get ideas that will help them in the classroom. The events can be easy ways to interact with international students and other scholars from across the globe.
- Americans should be aware of their own cultural lens and pay attention to whether they are expecting all students to know something that might be exclusive to U.S. culture.
- While most professors attend to verbal communication, non-verbal messages can be just as meaningful.

Resources

Boston University International Students & Scholars Office. "Tips for Successful Communication with International Students." 2010. June 15 2016 http://www.bu.edu/isso/files/pdf/Tips-Succesfull-Communication-Intl-Students.pdf

Michigan State University School of Journalism. "100 Questions and Answers About East Asian Cultures." Canton: Read the Spirit, 2014.

Michigan State University School of Journalism. "100 Questions and Answers About Immigrants to the U.S." Ann Arbor: Read the Spirit, 2016.

Ryan, Janette, ed. "Cross-Cultural Teaching and Learning for Home and International Students: Internationalisation, Pedagogy and Curriculum in Higher Education." New York: Routledge, 2012. Print.

—Palak Sabbineni is a communication major and public relations minor.

For international instructors, bridging languages is a process

"I know you are trying your hardest and it's not your fault, but I have a lot of trouble understanding what you're lecturing about because of your accent and the complexity of the English language. Mechanical engineering is hard enough, but it makes it a lot harder to learn these concepts when I can't understand what you're saying."

"Some redneck in my chem class: 'I picked this professor cuz his name sounded American but now I wish I had one of them foreign professors.'"

"I value and actually enjoy foreign professors for subjects that incorporate global perspectives and that are conducive to many views ..."

Students who have trouble with instructors' accents frequently post about their difficulties on social media. The problem seems most frequent in the sciences, technology, math and engineering. Professors who teach those subjects come from all over the world, and English is not everyone's first language. In many cases, students have to learn challenging material and have even more difficulty because of the language barrier.

For example, a Kent State University student posted that, when choosing classes, if the name of the teacher "looks foreign enough, and I think that they're not going to be able to speak English well enough for me to understand it, learn it and pass with a good grade, then I don't want to take that chance." Professors have reported that classes fill up faster when the listed instructors have names that seem American.

Accents run two ways. Just as students have trouble understanding some instructors' lectures, some instructors have trouble understanding students' questions. This limits the instructor's ability to answer questions completely in class.

Of course, misunderstandings aren't exclusive to language barriers. There are many cases where students can't get satisfying answers and language has nothing to do with it.

Cultural differences in teaching and learning styles can make it difficult to learn, too. However, international perspectives, when delivered well, can be an asset for a foreign-born professor.

International professors are hired for their knowledge and experience. If the university interviewed them and hired them, there must be potential for teaching success.

Strategies

In "Hidden Roads: Nonnative English-Speaking International Professors in the Classroom: New Directions for Teaching and Learning," Gust A. Yep suggests reframing the issue from one of language deficit to one of cultural enrichment. By bringing unique perspectives to the lesson, rather than trying to match English speakers lesson for lesson and word for word, international instructors bring unique advantages to their teaching and engage students in other ways.

University of Wyoming professor Chia-Fang (Sandy) Hsu is from Taiwan and teaches communication apprehension and cross-cultural studies. She also wrote for "Hidden Roads" and stated, "A teacher's willingness to work out problems with individual students, coupled with openness to students' ideas and criticism, should help improve students' negative attitudes toward the teacher."

Yunjuan Luo, a professor from China in the College of Media and Communication at Texas Tech, wrote that her communications students have high standards for her English, so she practices every day. According to Luo, differences in language, experience and culture have made it more difficult to understand and relate to her students. She has had such a different upbringing than many of her students that she really had to work to be able to connect to them.

Sun Young Lee, a public relations professor from South Korea, told The Hub at Texas Tech that the most challenging part of American culture was not the language, but learning American football and politics. Learning those helped her relate to and communicate with students.

Resources

Crump, Morgan. "Foreign Professors, Students Fight Language Barriers." The Texas Tech Hub, Nov. 20, 2012. June 13, 2016 http://www.ttuhub.net/2012/11/foreign-professors-students-fight-language-barriers/

Hendrix, Katherine Grace, and Aparna Hebbani, eds. "Hidden Roads: Nonnative English-Speaking International Professors in the Classroom." San Francisco: Jossey-Bass, New Directions for Teaching and Learning, 2014.

—*Matthew Hus is an advertising major and public relations minor.*

For those new to the language, English can be a sentence

"Thank you for always giving me a platform to speak comfortably in class even though English is not my first language."

"I hate the fact that because I am African you assumed that it is OK when I make an English mistake because English is my 'second language' even though I've practiced English my whole life."

It is always tricky teaching students for whom English is a second language because there are different degrees of proficiency and different types of English. Some international students find it intimidating to speak in English in front of classmates and the professor.

Culture also affects the way we communicate in a classroom. Phil Huelsbeck, a professor in international education at the University of Wisconsin-Eau Claire, writes that students from different cultures may have different "pause times" in response to different questions. He writes, "For instance, some international students may be accustomed to pausing for up to 30 seconds before responding to an instructor's question (to indicate to the instructor that the student is not taking the question lightly and giving it proper consideration)."

In cases like these, professors unfamiliar with the culture might feel pressure to save a student by respectfully excusing the student and asking for another student's opinion. A quick deflection may embarrass a student or make them feel rejected.

Other students speak British English, which is taught all over the world, and has constructions, words and spellings that do not coincide with American English. Huelsbeck wrote that professors might assess such variations as being incorrect. He wrote, "Words and phrases that at first glance may seem awkward or incorrect to a U.S. instructor may simply be the British variant in action. For instance, it may not be uncommon for a U.S. instructor to indicate that certain words like 'Aeroplane' are misspelled on an international student's paper."

One student who learned English in her native India before coming to college in the United States was told by a professor that her English was "colonial" and that most of her mistakes were due to the influences of her British and Indian English education. She was shocked and found the comment to be derogatory. She grew up in an English-speaking home, her education had all been in English, and she had taught high school for years. She had assumed that people would understand the differences in English from Anglophone countries. She was disappointed that her professor did not advise her early and in a culturally sensitive way about writing American English in her paper and had not directed her toward editing resources and tools.

Strategies

The student who came from India is Zilka Joseph, now a poet who has written two chapbooks, "Lands I Live In," "What Dread," and a book, "Sharp Blue Search of Flame," published by Wayne State University Press. She has taught at Oakland Community College, Washtenaw Community College, and was a graduate student assistant at the University of Michigan. Currently she teaches creative writing in Ann Arbor. As a college instructor, when she encounters writing issues similar to what she had, she makes her students aware of the different kinds of English in Anglophone countries and reassures them. She explains to international students and first-generation immigrant students that they need to familiarize themselves with American English and use it, especially when writing a formal document or academic paper. With examples from her own life, she teaches them how to use writers' handbooks and online resources to edit their work and makes them proud that they know more than one kind of English.

Dustin Carnahan, an associate professor in the Communications Department at Michigan State University, said some students have been speaking English for only a short time and struggle with some of its basic qualities, while others have a strong command of the language. He explained that the first thing he does is assess how well students can speak and understand English based on class discussions and early writing assignments. For students that he identifies as being comparatively new to English, Carnahan puts extra effort into critiquing their assignments, adding help for basic concepts like syntax and sentence structure. He treats second-language learners with a good command of English more or less like native English speakers.

In situations where cultural differences influence students' different communication styles such as longer pause times, Carnahan suggests waiting for students to deliver their thoughts. "I will usually follow up with these students when they say something that may be difficult to understand given their language limitations. A tactic I often use is to rephrase the student's contribution using different terms, and then ask the student if that is what they are trying to say so that the rest of the class might be able to see the value of their contribution as well," Carnahan said.

In "Teaching International Students: Improving Learning for All," Kam Louie from the University of Hong Kong wrote that teachers have to develop a meta-cultural sensitivity and awareness for international students. Louie wrote, "While it is helpful to gather bits and pieces of cultural knowledge, in the end, it is one's attitude and empathy towards the whole idea of cultural differences that matters."

Many campuses have resources that can help international students communicate more precisely. One resource might be an English language center that works with students who speak English as a second (or third) language by assessing and building language skills.

Patricia Walters, an associate director at the English Language Center at Michigan State University, advised:

- Consider what kind of language assumptions you make. This is really difficult for instructors who have little experience working with second-language learners, or those who have not had a second-language learning experience themselves.
- Write important points and instructions so that students stronger in reading but weaker in listening will be able to process the information.
- Consider asking diligent students to describe what vocabulary they find difficult, as well as other language factors regarding the class, such as cultural issues that arise in group work or speaking up during class. Use this information to improve how information is provided to students who need language help.

Walters said the center has found that when information is conveyed more clearly for the benefit of English learners, native English speakers benefit, too.

Resources

Harklau, Linda, Kay M. Losey, and Meryl Siegal, eds. "Generation 1.5 Meets College Composition: Issues in the Teaching of Writing to U.S.-Educated Learners of ESL." New York: Routledge, 1999.

Kisch, Marian. "Helping Faculty Teach International Students." International Educator: 2014.

Louie, Kam. "Teaching International Students: Improving Learning for All." New York: Routledge, 2005.

—Nichole Igwe is a journalism major and a public relations and French minor.

Gender and identity

Sexism means women lead men in numbers but still trail in power

"I wish my professor would stop the boys in the classroom who continuously talk over the women when they start to answer a question. It's like their booming voices overpower us and grab all of his attention and he immediately forgets I was talking, like what I had to say wasn't as important."

"I had a teacher who looked one of my female classmates in the eye and told her she couldn't have drawn something as good as she had because she was a woman, and that she should stop getting boys to do her work for her."

Women have the numbers on campus, but they don't have equal clout.

According to the The National Center for Education Statistics, women fill nearly 60 percent of the seats at colleges and their majority is growing. The center projects that, by 2024, there will be 15 million men in college and 20 million women. While the majority of college students are women, the majority of professors are not. The Chronicle of Higher Education has described a gender inequity pyramid in which women were half the faculty at community colleges, 41 percent at universities that grant bachelor's and master's degrees and only a third at doctoral-level institutions.

One woman told the website Mic, "In some of my male-dominated classes, I have noticed that male students tend to interrupt female students more than their male peers, and they mansplain basic concepts to them."

A University of Washington study suggested in 2016 that female students are more likely to leave science, technology, engineering and math because their male peers undermine their confidence. The study of 1,700 students found that males in undergraduate biology courses consistently ranked male classmates' knowledge of content as better than that of higher-scoring women. The women showed no such bias. Professors also observed men to be more outspoken in class. Lead author Dan Grunspan noticed that when men formed study groups, they also saw each other as being more competent. "Something is going on in the classroom that is either being influenced by currently held implicit biases or that is helping build implicit biases. We need to be thinking about what that means for the future," said Grunspan.

A 2015 Voices of Diversity report at Harvard said some female students reported that faculty and other students demeaned their intelligence. Some said professors called on them far less often than they called on men. Some female students said the absence of women as instructors and in course material made them feel marginalized.

In the fall of 2017, Harvard will start limiting privileges for student members of unauthorized, off-campus single-gender "final clubs." They have long been accused of perpetuating sexism and have been associated with higher levels of assault. By a wide majority, the clubs are men-only.

College sexism flourishes online, too. University of Virginia researchers found in an anonymous campus website in 2011-2013 that women as well as men "embraced extreme and alarming sexist language that objectifies and hypersexualizes women ... the vast majority of them found the ranking of women by appearance and sexual prowess commonplace and of little concern."

Researchers suggest that campus sexism is widespread. The most disturbing manifestation, sexual assaults, appear to be rising. A National Public Radio analysis of data from the U.S. Department of Education showed a 49 percent increase in campus sexual assaults between 2008 and 2012. Most assaults were against women. Some of the increase, but not all of it, appears to be caused by greater willingness to report assaults. In a 2015 Inside Higher Ed survey, 32 percent of college presidents agreed that sexual assault is a problem on U.S. campuses, but only 6 percent said it was a problem on their own campuses.

Female professors are not insulated from gender bias, as evidenced by fewer opportunities, lower wages and poorer ratings by students. At some colleges, student ratings are the only way in which teaching is evaluated.

Strategies

Although campus sexism extends far beyond the classroom walls, professors can reduce gender bias in their classrooms.

- Start by getting a baseline with Harvard's online and anonymous Implicit Bias test. https://implicit.harvard.edu/implicit/
- Set classroom behavior guidelines at the start of the term, stressing mutual respect and the ways in which students can enter in or will be brought into class discussions. Watch for interrupters early and establish your protocol for intervention.
- Distribute the chances to participate, bringing in the quiet students. Watch for subtle cues that show people have something to say. Don't immediately call on the first person who raises a hand.
- Call students by name. Repeat their best discussion points to reinforce them.
- Evaluate comments on content, not volume or style. Point attention to the thought behind the comment rather than the delivery.
- When doing small-group work or group projects, create integrated teams.

- Get to know students individually and learn about their needs for affirmation and feedback. Remain aware that students' needs are different.
- Check the diversity of sourcing in the material you use and in guest speakers.
- Observe differences in responses to styles of teaching situations and use multiple approaches. Men, on average, have been found to perform more confidently in classroom environments and women generally do better online. Use both, if you can, to give everyone chances to excel and to learn.

Resources

Paquette, Danielle. "The Remarkably Different Answers Men and Women Give When Asked Who's the Smartest in the Class." The Washington Post, Feb. 16, 2016.

Roman, Renee. "Gender Issues in Teaching: Does Nurturing Academic Success in Women Mean Rethinking Some of What We Do in the Classroom?" Stanford University Newsletter on Teaching, 1994. June 13, 2016 http://web.stanford.edu/dept/CTL/Newsletter/gender.pdf

Yang, Yan, YoonJung Cho, and Angela Watson. "Classroom Motivational Climate in Online and Face-to-Face Undergraduate Courses: The Interplay of Gender and Course Format." International Journal of E-Learning & Distance Education, 2015. June 13, 2016 http://www.ijede.ca/index.php/jde/article/view/890

—Brittany Dreon is an advertising and public relations major.

Helping students break
career-based gender stereotypes

"Thank you for recognizing that I am a student who cares about my education, regardless of my gender."

"Sexist engineering professor? Check! Welcome to the real world of women in Science. Good thing I can keep up with the boys ;)"

It can be daunting for students to break into fields where they seem to be defying gender stereotypes. There is a major effort to get women to major in STEM (Science, Technology, Engineering and Math) because, historically, those industries are male-dominated. In 2014, only 7.2 percent of mechanical engineers, 27.9 percent of environmental scientist/geoscientists, and 39 percent of chemists were women, according to the U.S. Bureau of Labor Statistics report "Women in the Labor Force." Often, women are greeted with disbelief, bias and skepticism that they can do the work in STEM fields. Men defy gender stereotypes in nursing, elementary and middle school teaching, clinical science, physical therapy, social work and other fields. Supportive professors can help students make a successful journey through gender bias.

Knowing how to address gender bias is vital to helping all students feel confident in their career paths.

A female computer science student reported feeling frustrated when her professor referred only to "he" or "him" when speaking of generic computer scientists. She said, "I subconsciously think that computer scientists are or should only be males."

Similarly, engineering majors have noticed that it is rarer for women to have prior knowledge of cars and power. One female student said, "Sometimes professors assume that we know more technical terms, especially on the topic of cars, than we actually do. Dads take their sons to look under the hood, not their daughters, unfortunately." Chances are that not every student in class, male or female, has prior knowledge of what is being referenced in the lesson. Employ base-level assessment and training on mechanics in entry-level engineering classes to make sure everyone starts with the same understanding of basic concepts.

While instructors are responsible for classroom atmosphere, they are not the only ones who influence it. If men don't like having women in class with them, the experience for everyone can be incredibly unpleasant. Many students said that often when they must create work groups, they tend to cluster by gender. If instructors mix the groups, everyone will gain experience working across gender lines.

Strategies

The student who wrote the first quote above felt her teacher did a wonderful job making her and other women feel included. She said it was "the little things" the professor did that created a good class environment.

Ryan Sweeder, associate professor of chemistry in Lyman Briggs College at Michigan State University and a science education researcher, emphasizes "the little things."

- Sweeder suggests instructors who describe hypothetical situations use both male and female. He said, "If you have a scenario, what name do you use? Do you use a male name or a female name? Almost always now I'll use a female name … for that exact reason."

- Professors who refer to work and research by professionals of different genders highlight gender diversity in the field, whatever the subject.

- When teaching the history of a field where not many women have been involved, professors can explain why they are not being noted. Teachers can use the lack of role models to encourage women to make history. Inspiring women to make their names known tells them they are respected and are expected to make as many advances as men.

- Sweeder discourages instructors from making it a point to tell women how wonderful it is that they picked a career in a STEM major. The sentiment is nice in principle, but can appear as belittling, broaden the gap between genders and make women feel discredited.
- He encourages students to join clubs for STEM majors, including organizations for women. When women mentor other women, it can boost confidence. Helping students find their careers or information about them is a classic way to show interest in students' futures and engage them in the learning.

Kristin Parent, an assistant professor in the Department of Biochemistry and Molecular Biology at Michigan State University, combats gender stereotyping in these ways:

Parent said that some women feel anxious about joining STEM fields because, "There's less women in the higher levels, so there are less role models that they can see having a positive impact." She suggests leading by example. She said the more women that get leadership roles and lead by example, the more comfortable female students will feel.

Parent takes an anticipatory approach, telling her classes about biases in the industries that they wish to enter and how they can deal with co-workers who exhibit actions implying negative stereotypes. "I try to mentor my students on how to get into situations that would not be biased."

Occasionally, some students exhibit gender bias. Parent recommends that instructors handle this head-on. In one instance, she told a student that if he did not improve his behavior, she would report him to the dean. She said, "It's good for the surrounding students to see that you're taking care of the situation and that you're going to talk to the student about inappropriate behavior. Making a stance that you don't stand for that behavior is important."

Resources

Pittman, Olivia. "7 Organizations Working to Promote Women in STEM." College Raptor. June 13, 2016 https://www.collegeraptor.com/blog/higher-education/7-organizations-working-to-promote-women-in-stem/

Sheehy, Kelsey. "Colleges Work to Retain Women in STEM Majors." US News, July 1, 2013.

—Alexandria Drzazgowski is a professional writing major and Spanish minor.

Breaking the binary: Seeing sexuality as a spectrum

"Get to know me, support me and all of my nuances and differences, but once you do, don't treat me like the token gay student."

It is common for students to remain anonymous in a lecture-based course, and often their sexuality is ambiguous to professors. Ambiguity, however, is not the issue. It is how lesbian, bisexual, gay, trans, and queer (LGBTQ) students are treated.

The student quoted above described varying reactions to class experiences. At times, her identity as a lesbian remained unknown, and she said that did not bother her. Other times, her orientation was clear to the entire class, which resulted in her being treated as "the token gay student." She felt she had to explain, or even defend, her identity. While professors may believe they are encouraging lively classroom discussion, distancing an LGBTQ student from the rest of the class may be isolating. Comments about a student's sexuality implying the student is outside the norm can diminish feelings of safety and comfort that encourage learning.

It is crucial for instructors to help students see beyond a sexual binary: male or female, gay or straight. All students are equal, no matter where they fall on the spectrum. This graphic, created with permission from The Trevor Project, shows how sexual identity is fluid and cannot be confined by just

Sexuality on a spectrum

While many believe that gender identity and sexual identity remain in binary, organzations such as The Trevor Project have advocated for a fluid approach to understanding the role of gender and sexual identity. The spectrums below serve as a guide to help determine where one might fall in regards to several facets of their identity.

Biological sex
(What the doctor assigned at birth)

Male   Intersex   Female

Gender identity
(What you feel about your gender)

Man   Genderfluid/Trans*   Woman
Female to Male (FTM)   Genderqueer   Male to Female (MTF)

Gender Expression
(How you present yourself to others)

Masculine   Androgynous   Feminine
Non-binary

Gender Presentation
(How the world sees you)

Man   Transgender   Woman
Genderqueer/Non-binary

Sexual Orientation
(Who you're attracted to)

Attracted to   Bisexual/Pansexual   Attracted to
women   Asexual   men

illustration by Matthew Hus   source: The Trevor Project

two terms. The Trevor Project is a national organization that provides crisis intervention and suicide prevention services to LGBTQ individuals ages 13-24.

Deanna "Dee" Hurlbert, director of the LGBTQ Resource Center at Michigan State University, said heterosexuality is treated as the standard in how some classes are framed or delivered. College applications, studies and forms often ask people to identify as male or female with no room for anything else. Marriages and attraction are usually defined as heterosexual. These unintentional slights are called microaggressions.

Psychology Today describes microaggressions as "verbal or nonverbal and environmental slights, snubs, or insults, whether intentional or unintentional, which communicate hostile, derogatory, or negative messages to target persons based solely upon their marginalized group membership." Microaggressions are often directed at members of the LGBTQ community and racial groups.

Hurlbert suggests professors avoid references to gender or sexuality when they are not relevant to prevent assumptions, misspeaking or distancing students.

"There might be some folks who just don't want to touch on sexuality at all and at the same time, when that happens they don't see how they are normalizing one sexuality over another." She says this can make people who are not heterosexual feel invisible.

A gay student described his experiences with professors as mostly positive, but noted that his orientation was omitted in classroom discussions, even when it was relevant to material such as metaphors and literary techniques and events in history. Sexual orientation has been a theme in many works of literature and has sometimes influenced policy.

Whether professors dodge the topic of sexuality or accidentally offend, there are strategies that can help make all students feel welcome.

Strategies

Why are sexuality and gender such tricky topics in the classroom? For starters, the spectrum is diverse and the language is changing. New terms emerge and others disappear. For instance, Hurlbert explained that younger generations are reclaiming the once rejected umbrella term "queer." She said the term "is inclusive of those who might not want to identify with a particular label, or for those still in the process of figuring themselves out."

Another piece of the puzzle is that many students are questioning who they are and questioning who they are attracted to. This is why inclusive language is critical. Here are some strategies professors can employ to avoid normalizing heterosexuality and to prevent excluding LGBTQ students.

Preparation: Professors can start by educating themselves. They can commit time to understanding sexual orientation beyond the binary scale. Does the university provide resources to LGBTQ students? Refer students to the appropriate office when they seek help or information. Becoming well-versed in sexual orientation, gender and attraction prepares instructors for the variety of possibilities that can be relevant in lecture. There are sometimes workshops to help professors as well as students learn more.

In the moment: Educating one's self is only the beginning. The next step is to know how to act when issues arise in the classroom. This is the main take-home message: People should not assume anything about sexuality. Hurlbert said the Trevor Project chart shows that middle sexualities often get washed out. She gave this in-the-moment example:

"You can't assume, 'Oh, Genie says she has a boyfriend, so Genie must be heterosexual.' Genie might not be heterosexual, she could be bisexual, pansexual ... so the awareness helps, but let people tell their own stories and recognize when you are making assumptions."

Professors also have to be prepared to moderate microaggressions using strong facilitation skills. Hurlbert said professors can model speaking about students using their names, rather than gender-based pronouns like he or she. Refrain from labeling others or their behaviors with phrases like "you people," but also remember that terms such as "ladies and gentlemen," might not include everyone. Cultivate inclusivity. Terms like "class" and "students" mean everyone.

Follow-up: Hurlbert says it is important to have shame resilience. "When you misstep, allow yourself to feel guilty for unintentionally harming a student, but recognize how to act differently next time." Hurlbert describes the impact an apology can have. Sometimes we cannot completely right a wrong, but we can acknowledge that we were wrong. Apologizing is a productive way of moving forward. Hurlbert stressed the importance of apologizing without the expectation of immediate forgiveness. Recovery is a process. There will be many opportunities to regain trust.

Resources

"Coming Out as You." The Trevor Project. June 13, 2016 http://www.thetrevorproject.org/section/YOU

"The PFLAG National Glossary of Terms." PFLAG, Inc. June 13, 2016 https://www.pflag.org/glossary

Stewart, Dafina Lazarus, Kristen A. Renn, and G. Blue Brazelton. "Gender and Sexual Diversity in U.S. Higher Education: Contexts and Opportunities for LGBTQ College Students." San Francisco: Jossey-Bass, New Directions for Student Services, 2015.

—Natalie Kozma is an advertising major and public relations minor.

Transitioning on campus: Finding and redefining identity

"Your unswerving effort to validate and use my correct pronouns in class as well as making me feel like being referred to as the correct gender was something I am owed, not something

optional, made me feel safe, validated, and humanized. It meant the world to me."

"I dropped your class after you assumed my gender based on my appearance and voice. You split us up into (male and female) groups and made me feel like I had no place in the class and that my identity isn't real."

"When you respond to my explanation of my pronouns with your refusal to use them based on your opinion that they are 'grammatically incorrect' (which isn't true), you are saying your views on grammar are more important than my comfort, my safety, and me as a person."

Transitioning from one sexual identity to another on campus can be difficult. Redefining one's identity can range from choosing how to present one's self, to hormone therapy and surgery. Some people are gender-nonconforming or identify as having no gender. One difficulty that transgender students report is having professors who refuse to acknowledge their gender identity and name change because it doesn't match their student account information.

The student newspaper at Michigan State published a letter that said, "My sophomore year, I had a professor who didn't approve of my gender identity and made sure I was aware of how much he didn't like it. When I told him I prefer to go by my chosen name, Elliott, he called me by my birth name and argued about what my real name was. After class, I told him I prefer male pronouns because I was transgender and identified as a man. Instead, during class, he referred to me as a woman whenever he referenced something I said. When I or other students corrected him, he said, 'He? But you've got… you're a woman!' It shouldn't be acceptable for a professor to reference a student's breasts in class, especially as a way to deny someone's gender identity."

Members of state legislatures across the country debate what students may wear and which bathrooms and locker rooms they may use. According to "Transgender Issues on College Campuses," trans students "violate society's expectation that someone is either female or male, which makes them vulnerable to harassment and violence."

Strategies

Deanna Hurlbert, director of the LGBT Resource Center at Michigan State University, said "I think that one of the great disservices we do is when we're corrected, or redirected, or given information that we might disagree with. People can tend to shut down, feel defensive, and deflect, and minimize whatever it is that's coming at them. And I think people who are in positions of power, often intellectuals like faculty, might be more likely to do that."

Transgender issues are developing so rapidly that keeping up on language is a challenge. Even pronouns have become an issue. In English, personal pronouns have gender as in she, her, hers and he, him, his. Some people prefer to be identified with new, gender-neutral pronouns such as "ze" or "ve." Another alternative is "their." Some instructors say the singular "they" violates noun-pronoun agreement and mark it wrong. But the singular "they" has been with us since Chaucer. "They" as a gender-neutral pronoun was made Word of the Year in 2015 by the American Dialect Society, the year that the Washington Post allowed that usage and when The New York Times used the non-binary courtesy title Mx., pronounced "mix."

Hurlbert suggests professors remain open to the possibility of being wrong and examine how they see gender, to be humble and to listen. "Case law is increasingly telling us that individuals have a right to self determination and self expressions and that includes a right to define their sex for themselves, to name themselves, and the right to name how others will refer to them," Hurlbert adds. "So that includes how they define their bodies, regardless of whether or not they have a penis or a vagina or whatever manifestation of sexual parts, and they have a right to name and describe their gender and express that."

According to Hurlbert, trans students should also be open to the possibility of being wrong about their professors and to practice the platinum rule, to treat others as they want to be treated, not as you want to be treated. "If you put yourself in that person's shoes, what would you want, what would be your expectations for respect?" Hurlbert asked.

Resources

Beemyn, Brett, Billy Curtis, Masen Davis, and Nancy Jean Tubbs. "Transgender Issues on College Campuses." Wiley Online Library. Wiley, Sept. 8, 2005. June 13, 2016 http://vp.studentlife.uiowa.edu/assets/Transgender-Issues-on-College-Campuses.pdf

Howard, Kim, and Annie Stevens. "Out & About Campus: Personal Accounts by Lesbian, Gay, Bisexual & Transgender College Students." Los Angeles: Alyson, 2000.

Michigan State University School of Journalism. "100 Questions and Answers About Transgender People." Ann Arbor: Read the Spirit, 2016.

Sanlo, Ronni L. "Gender Identity and Sexual Orientation: Research, Policy, and Personal Perspectives." San Francisco: Jossey-Bass, 2005.

—Michelle Armstead is a journalism major with a specialization in business reporting and an economics major.

Finances

Hardly working or working too hard?
College debt weighs more than ever

"I wish that you would realize that I'm working hard to be in your class—both on my assignments to get a good grade, and at my job to be able to afford it."

In the 2015-2016 school year alone, tuition costs rose 2.9 percent, according to the College Board, faster than the rate of inflation. A 2.9 percent change does not seem like much, but 30 years of tuition increases that have exceeded inflation and wages have made it much harder to work oneself through college.

The Wall Street Journal reported that 70 percent of those receiving bachelor's degrees in 2015 also had student loan debts. The average debt load was slightly more than $35,000.

Randy Olson, a postdoctoral researcher at the University of Pennsylvania, provides insight into what it takes to work through college today. His research accounts for inflation, the change in the minimum wage, and the rise in tuition over 33 years. He calculates that while it once took nine hours a week to earn enough money to pay for college, the burden has become a 60-hour-a-week sentence. These numbers do not include food, transportation, clothing, social outings, or anything else necessary to the average college student. Basing expectations for today's students on what it was like when the professor went through college might be considerably out of date.

Georgetown researchers found that in 2015, employed students were working on average 30 hours a week. One working student said that her 65-hour-a-week work

Tuition, fees, room and board in 2015 dollars

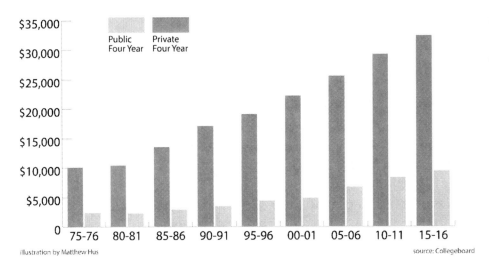

Public Four Year
Private Four Year

$35,000
$30,000
$25,000
$20,000
$15,000
$10,000
$5,000
0

75-76 80-81 85-86 90-91 95-96 00-01 05-06 10-11 15-16

illustration by Matthew Hus   source: Collegeboard

commitment hurt her studies. "I sleep about 3-4 hours a night, which affects my abilities to focus and succeed while I'm in class." Many students who must work to stay in college are unable to focus on classwork because of the time their jobs require. They have to fight to stay in college and to avoid huge debt.

Another student said work-shift requirements of the job that made it possible for her to be in college also made it impossible for her to take the 12 credits she needed to be a full-time student, or to graduate in four years.

A junior at Michigan State University admits to feeling like she is missing out on educational opportunities because of her job: "Sometimes I get jealous of my roommates without jobs that can actually study for hours on end for their exams."

Students with heavy work schedules can be judged to be less committed than those who don't need jobs. Sagging grades, odd schedules and sleepiness can be misinterpreted as a lack of interest when they are actually signs of desperately trying to succeed. On the job, some bosses are no less forgiving than professors about expecting top performance.

Strategies

While professors don't set tuition and can't make college affordable, they can help students work with financial realities.

Jonathan Ritz, a professor and academic adviser at Michigan State University, knows many students struggling to complete their credits and keep the demanding jobs that pay for them. From experience with a wide range of students, Ritz has discovered what he believes to be the most effective way to handle these student situations: "The most important thing is to be absolutely clear, quantitatively clear, about the impact attendance has on the grade." By giving students a detailed syllabus describing class activities and penalties for missing class and sticking to specifications, professors can help students plan their work schedules.

Ritz also said that being clear but understanding about late assignments can make a large difference in a working student's success. He said that a student who requests a deadline extension initiates a great teachable moment for that student's future. "In my syllabus, it says that you have to request a deadline extension 48 hours in advance," said Ritz. In this way, students must think ahead to their upcoming schedule, learn how to describe the issue, and articulate why an extension will lead to a better project. A clear policy in the syllabus at the beginning of the term is vital to the success of this strategy. This allows students a chance for extended deadlines if work becomes overwhelming, but prevents students from taking advantage of extensions.

Monica List, a professor and adviser for Bioethics, Humanities, and Society at Michigan State University, suggests professors provide action points to get students through the term. List said action points direct students to create a list of assignments for them to complete to pass the course with the highest grade possible but also keep them from drowning in work. "Students sometimes have to pick and choose what tasks or assignments they're going to complete from a course if they can't complete everything." On this list, mandatory assignments (if you miss, you can't pass) come first. Following this is the not mandatory, high-stakes assignments (those with higher points values), then anything else.

If the student is unable to complete all the assignments for the class, List also advises them to complete what comes easiest: "For some students, writing comes easy, for some students, they really struggle with that. Do first what comes easiest to you, but also consider how much it's worth." Assisting overworked students with setting priorities could be the difference between a pass and fail in the classroom.

List said some of her colleagues offer options for high-stakes assignments. In some cases, they will provide two options for midterms or finals. One option will be a sit-down test with multiple choice and short-answer questions. The other will be a take-home essay. In this way, students can work with their strengths to exhibit their knowledge of the subject, and working students can choose what fits better into their schedules. Students are still tested on what they have learned, but have choices about how to fit the assessment into their schedules.

Professors' role in the return on investment of a college education, however, is not in keeping costs down, but in raising the value. In 2015, Gallup and Purdue University collaborated on an Index Report called "Great Jobs, Great Lives. The Relationship Between Student Debt, Experiences and Perceptions of College Worth." It showed that fewer than 40 percent of 2006-2015 college grads said college was worth the money, compared to 50 percent of all alums. While this could be related to rising costs or how far along one is in a career, the difference is significant.

According to the Gallup-Purdue report, professors are key determinants in the perceived value of college. The grads were almost twice as likely to say that college was worth it if their professors cared about them as a person. Mentoring had as great a positive effect. This was followed closely by having at least one professor who made students feel excited about learning.

The report recommended that "All universities need to strongly emphasize the quality of the interactions faculty members have with students to maintain their promise of a valuable college education to prospective undergraduates. In many cases, quality interactions mean finding innovative ways to make professors more accessible and students' interactions with them more meaningful. In the longer run, it may mean shifting the institution's culture to give faculty members more incentive to hone their teaching practices or to make a talent for engaging students and supporting learning outcomes a more important part of hiring criteria for educators."

Resources

College Board Trends in Higher Education Reports. "College Prices Continue Moderate Rise, and Student Aid Remains Stable, Leading to Increased Net Prices." Nov. 4, 2015. June 13, 2016 https://www.collegeboard.org/releases/2015/college-board-trends-higher-education-reports-college-prices-moderate-rise-student-aid-stable-increased-net-prices

College Board Trends in Higher Education Reports. "Tuition and Fees and Room and Board over Time, 1975-76 to 2015-16, Selected Years." June 13, 2016 http://trends.collegeboard.org/college-pricing/figures-tables/tuition-and-fees-and-room-and-board-over-time-1975-76-2015-16-selected-years

Olson, Randy. "It's Impossible to Work Your Way Through College Nowadays." Blog: March 29, 2014. June 13, 2016 http://www.theatlantic.com/education/archive/2014/04/the-myth-of-working-your-way-through-college/359735/

Rapacon, Stacy. "More College Students Are Working While Studying." CNBC, Oct. 29, 2015.

—*Alexandria Drzazgowski is a professional writing major and Spanish minor.*

Texts and supplemental materials can be expensive and seem superfluous

"I have already dug myself thousands of dollars into debt to have the opportunity to take your class. I would rather not spend even more money on homework programs or excessively expensive textbooks just to be able to pass it."

"It bothers me when you joke that you are requiring us to buy your book because you will get royalties from it."

Over the course of an undergraduate career, the average student will spend almost $5,000 on textbooks and supplemental materials, according to The College Board.

Requiring that students have only the latest edition of a book or access to online programs drives up their costs. New-edition requirements keep students off the used-book market and prevent them from passing books along. In some cases, the latest is the greatest, but the California state auditor reported in 2008 that in most instances, changes between textbook editions are minuscule.

One student recalls being frustrated because the $300 textbook she bought was used only a few times in class throughout the term: "It is disheartening to me that the book that I bought was only used twice over the course of a 15-week period." This is a frequent complaint among students. Having purchased books they never used as first-year students, some sophomores wait until the last minute to buy books because they know some professors won't get to all the books on the course list.

According to a report endorsed by The American Association of University Professors ethics committee, "Because professors sometimes realize profits from sales to their students (although, more often than not, the profits are trivial or nonexistent), professors may seem to be inappropriately enriching themselves at the expense of their students."

"Campus Grotto: The Inside Source at College" polled 1,000 students about their top complaints. High on the list was the cost of textbooks. Lower were professors who write books and require their students to buy them.

Professors sometimes write books because there is nothing comparable on the market. But students are simply upset with the cost of materials on top of what they are already paying for college. One individual states, "As a student who pays for college without financial assistance from my parents, I find it angering to spend such a large amount of money on textbooks."

Any costs can contribute to the expense or debt loads that cause some students to suspend their studies or take on large loans. While professors don't set tuition or textbook costs, they can take a nick out of that $5,000 materials bill.

Strategies

Helping students with their expenses starts with being conscientious about the price of required materials.

Michigan State professor Monica List said that in many cases, online versions and PDFs of books are cheaper than print copies. She said, "not everything comes in this format, but it's very convenient. All students can be logged on and looking at the book at the same time." Allowing students the option to access these media can cut down on prices immensely. Additionally, professors can allow older editions of required books, filling in where updates are needed.

MSU professor and adviser Jon Ritz advises that texts be required only if they enhance the classroom experience throughout the term. If a textbook is used for only a few days, it should be evaluated on what it really brings to class discussion. If the information is non-essential or is essentially covered in other books, the instructor can cut it and save students money.

If only small sections are required from each text a professor is thinking of assigning, creating a course pack may be a great choice. Tyler Smeltekop, course materials program manager at Michigan State, says his goal is to "package class content in a convenient, attractive, and cost-effective way." University libraries and course-pack companies have people to negotiate licensing with publishers for materials that a professor requests. Each article, photograph or chapter is approved by the publisher and then printed in a customized pack for the classroom. This process can be completed with almost any material, including content from overseas publishers. Cost depends on the size of the pack, normally at a per-page rate. Smeltekop says a course pack with one chapter of a book could cost $1.50 versus buying the entire book for $10-12.

Professors who want to create their own materials no longer have to use traditional methods with the large markups that come from publishing houses, marketers, shippers and bookstores. Professors can self-publish now through a host of print-on-demand publishers that print only the desired quantity and deliver books at a lower cost to students with a royalty that is set by the author/publisher. In many cases, professors can publish cheaper book for a higher royalty by self-publishing.

Some university libraries have Espresso Book Machines, which can print original books or classics for student purchase.

Some companies have been reluctant to list their newer titles on book machines, but professors can still become publishers of their own work. The Espresso Book Machine website by On Demand Books lists available titles and sites.

There is no escaping the fact that college is expensive and that professors didn't make it that way. But with thoughtfulness and planning, they can lessen the bite.

Resources

California Bureau of State Audits. "Affordability of College Textbooks: Textbook Prices Have Risen Significantly in the Last Four Years, but Some Strategies May Help to Control These Costs for Students." Sacramento: California State Auditor, Bureau of State Audits, 2008.

Kingkade, Tyler. "College Textbook Prices Increasing Faster Than Tuition and Inflation." The Huffington Post: Jan. 4, 2013. June 13, 2016 http://www.huffingtonpost.com/2013/01/04/college-textbook-prices-increase_n_2409153.html

"On Professors Assigning Their Own Texts to Students." American Association of University Professors, November 2004. June 13, 2016 https://www.aaup.org/report/professors-assigning-their-own-texts-students

—Alexandria Drzazgowski is a professional writing major and Spanish minor.

Selected bibliography

Ackerman, Robert, David DiRamio, and Regina L. Garza Mitchell. "Creating a Veteran-Friendly Campus: Strategies for Transition and Success." San Francisco: Jossey-Bass, 2009.

Ambrose, Susan A., et al. "How Learning Works: Seven Research-Based Principles for Smart Teaching." San Francisco: Jossey-Bass, 2010.

Angelo, Thomas A., and K. Patricia Cross. "Classroom Assessment Techniques: A Handbook for College Teachers." San Francisco: Jossey-Bass, 1993.

Barkley, Elizabeth F. "Student Engagement Techniques: A Handbook for College Faculty." San Francisco: Jossey-Bass, 2010.

Barkley, Elizabeth F., K. Patricia Cross, and Claire Howell Major. "Collaborative Learning Techniques: A Handbook for College Faculty." San Francisco: Jossey-Bass, 2004.

Burgstahler, Sheryl, and Michael K. Young. "Universal Design in Higher Education: From Principles to Practice, 2nd ed." Cambridge: Harvard Education Press, 2015.

Brophy, Jere. "Teaching." International Academy of Education, UNESCO and International Bureau of Education. Chicago: University of Illinois, n.d.

Carey, Benedict. "How We Learn: The Surprising Truth about When, Where, and Why it Happens." New York: Random House, 2015 reprint.

Cashin, William E. "Effective Classroom Discussions. Idea Paper #49." The IDEA Center. 2011. June 13, 2016 http:// ideaedu.org/wp-content/uploads/2014/11/IDEA_Paper_49. pdf

Dalke, Anne French. "Teaching to Learn/Learning to Teach: Meditations on the Classroom." New York: Peter Lang, 2002.

Davis, Barbara Gross. "Tools for Teaching. 2nd ed." San Francisco: Jossey-Bass, 1993.

Falk, Erika. "Becoming a New Instructor: A Guide for College Adjuncts and Graduate Students." New York: Routledge, 2012.

Fox, Helen. "When Race Breaks Out: Conversations about Race and Racism in College Classrooms." New York: Peter Lang, 2001.

Hopkins, Katy. "6 Challenges for International Students in College." New York: U.S. News & World Report. 28 August 2012.

"How to Assist Emotionally Distressed Students. Tips for Faculty/Staff." California State University Organization of Counseling Center Directors in Higher Education by Committee on Campus Mental Health. June 13, 2016 http://psyservs.sfsu.edu/sites/sites7.sfsu.edu.psyservs/files/assets/PDF_Files/HowtoAssist.pdf

Howard, Jay R., and Maryellen Weimer. "Discussion in the College Classroom: Getting Your Students Engaged and Participating in Person and Online." San Francisco: Jossey-Bass, 2015.

Jones, Frederic H., Brian T. Jones, and Patrick Jones. "Fred Jones Tools for Teaching: Discipline, Instruction, Motivation, 2nd ed." Santa Cruz: Frederic H. & Associates, 2007.

Landis, Kay, ed. "Start Talking: A Handbook for Engaging Difficult Dialogues in Higher Education." Anchorage: University of Alaska and Alaska Pacific University, 2008. June 13, 2016 http://www.difficultdialoguesuaa.org/handbook

Lang, James M. "On Course: A Week-by-Week Guide to Your First Semester of College Teaching." Cambridge: Harvard University Press, 2008.

McKeachie, Wilbert J., and Marilla Svinicki. "McKeachie's Teaching Tips: Strategies, Research, and Theory for College and University Teachers, 14th ed." Independence: Wadsworth Publishing (Cengage), 2013.

Morrison, Gary R., Steven M. Ross, and Jerrold E. Kemp. "Designing Effective Instruction." Hoboken: John Wiley & Sons, 2004.

Sarkisian, Ellen. "Teaching American Students: A Guide for International Faculty and Teaching Assistants in Colleges and Universities." Cambridge: Harvard University Derek Bok Center for Teaching and Learning, 2006.

Saunders, Shari, and Diana Kardia. "Creating Inclusive College Classrooms." Ann Arbor: University of Michigan Center for Research on Learning and Teaching. June 13, 2016 http://crlt.umich.edu/gsis/p3_1

Yelon, Stephen L. "Powerful Principles of Instruction." White Plains: Longman USA, 1996.